simple food

text and photographs
by Jill Dupleix

whitecap

simple food

Jill Dupleix

notes
Measurements are given in standard
U.S. cups and spoons. All recipe ideas
serve 4 unless otherwise suggested.
All eggs are free-range and large; all
herbs are fresh; all salt is sea salt,
and all pepper is freshly ground black
pepper unless otherwise stated.

Creative Director Mary Evans
with design assistance from
Rachel Gibson and Katy Davis
Project Editors Janet Illsley and
Norma MacMillan
Production Nancy Roberts

First published in 2002 by
Quadrille Publishing Limited
Alhambra House
27-31 Charing Cross Road
London WC2H 0LS

Published in Canada in 2002 by
Whitecap Books
For more information, please contact
Whitecap Books,
351 Lynn Avenue, North Vancouver,
BC, V7J 2C4

ISBN 1 55285 365 9
Printed in Singapore

contents

Manifesto *I call this simple food for complicated people.*

It's all about how to get home tonight, have a glass of wine, and be eating something delicious – fast roast fish, little ham and egg pies, or parmesan lamb chops – within half an hour. It's also about slow food that cooks itself, such as figs and baked ricotta, or baked potato with blue cheese. And food that's almost patronizingly easy, as in the world's simplest recipe for creamy banana ice cream.

I love to cook, but I don't want to be cooking when I could be eating and drinking. My food philosophy – indeed, my entire philosophy – is to get away with doing as little as possible, as often as possible, by keeping things simple.

If you have great ingredients at their best, you can get away with doing less to them. There is no need for artificiality, because the real thing is good enough.

With *Simple Food*, techniques are everyday, tools are basic, and flavors are real. It's a way of getting the food part of your life under control, so that it does what it's meant to do – makes you feel good.

Simple, really.

simple starters

Sweetcorn shot soup

You won't believe how sweet this is. The trick is making the base stock with the stripped corn cobs, then adding the corn kernels for more flavor. Serve as a first course, or pour into shot glasses and serve as a chic appetizer with drinks.

Shuck the ears of corn, and discard the leaves and those pesky fine strings. Using a sharp knife, shear off the kernels and set aside. Place the corn cobs in a pan, cover with the cold water, add salt, and simmer for 30 minutes, then strain, reserving the broth.

Mince the onion. Melt the butter in a pan, and cook the onion for 5 minutes. Add the corn kernels and the strained stock, and simmer for 15 minutes. Whiz the soup in a blender until smooth, then strain through a fine sieve, pressing the juices through with a wooden spoon.

To serve, gently reheat the soup, whisk in the cream, salt, pepper, and nutmeg, and simmer for 2 minutes. Serve hot, warm, or chilled. This quantity will fill 4 soup bowls or 10 small shot glasses.

SERVES 4

4 ears of corn

$1\frac{1}{2}$ quarts cold water

sea salt

1 onion, peeled

1 tbsp butter

1 tbsp cream

freshly ground black pepper

$\frac{1}{4}$ tsp ground nutmeg

Tuna and white bean toast

Whiz 1 cup drained, canned white beans and 7 oz canned tuna with its oil in a blender. Add 2 anchovy fillets, black pepper, and lemon juice, and whiz again. Serve on toasted sourdough bread smeared with garlicky olive oil, with black olives and thyme on top.

Chipolata oysters

Cold oysters are great on their own, but they are even better with hot little sausages on the side. Take a bite of a hot, peppery beef sausage, then slurp down a cold, salty, tangy oyster. Repeat until nothing is left.

Scrub the oysters well. Wrap a thick dish towel around your left hand and hold an oyster firmly in your palm, the flat side facing upward, the thin, pointy end toward you. Push the point of the knife firmly through the hinge, feeling your way, twisting the blade slightly and increasing the pressure until you feel it give way.

Wipe the blade free of any grit, and run it neatly under the top shell. Lift off the top shell, but keep the oyster steady so you don't lose its natural juices. Loosen the oyster from its shell and set the shell down on a bed of watercress or parsley. Repeat to open the rest of the oysters.

Lightly oil a nonstick frying pan. Prick the sausages well and pan-fry them gently, turning once or twice. When they are sizzling hot and cooked through, drain them on paper towel and arrange next to the oysters. Add the lime or lemon quarters and serve, with flutes of Champagne or tankards of beer.

SERVES 4
12 large, fresh oysters
watercress or parsley sprigs
16 small, spicy, fresh beef
sausages (chipolatas)
1 lime or lemon, quartered

Anchoïade toasts

Provençal anchovy paste has a strong and sunny flavor that makes it the perfect appetizer to have on toasted baguette with drinks in the sunshine. It is also delicious on hard-boiled eggs, or drizzled over roasted vegetables.

Using a mortar and pestle, pound the anchovies, tomato paste, and garlic until smooth. Add the olive oil, drop by drop to begin with as you continue to pound, until you have a thick paste. Then add the oil by the teaspoonful, until the mixture is smooth and glossy. Beat in the orange juice and some pepper.

Finely slice the baguette into 20 or so slices, and toast on both sides under the broiler until dry and golden. (You can do all this in advance.) Spoon a little anchoiade onto each toast to serve.

SERVES 6 TO 8

24 canned anchovy fillets in oil
   (2 small cans), drained

2 tbsp tomato paste

2 garlic cloves, peeled

4–5 tbsp extra virgin olive oil

1 tbsp orange juice

freshly ground black pepper

1 baguette

Spiced quail eggs

Boil 12 quail eggs in simmering water for 3 minutes. Cool in cold water, then peel and trim a slice off one end so they sit up. Dip the pointy end in smoked paprika and top with a flake of sea salt. Serve with drinks.

Tomato and basil bruschetta

Summer cooking is simple. Get up in the morning, do this to a few ripe tomatoes, leave them to infuse, and go back to bed. The first course is almost done.

Cut out the cores from the tomatoes and cut a small cross at the base. Dunk them in a pot of boiling water for 20 seconds, then peel off the skins. Cut the tomatoes in half, squeeze out and discard the seeds and juice, and roughly chop the flesh.

Lightly toss the tomatoes in a bowl with the garlic cloves, basil leaves, sea salt, pepper, and olive oil. Cover and set aside in a cool place to infuse. Do this an hour or two before you intend to eat.

When ready to serve, toast the bread on both sides. Dip a pastry brush in the tomato marinade and brush each toast. Pile the tomatoes and basil on top, drizzle with the juices, and serve.

SERVES 4

4 ripe, red tomatoes

2 garlic cloves, peeled and smashed

1 cup basil leaves

sea salt

freshly ground black pepper

4 tbsp extra virgin olive oil

4 thick slices sourdough bread

Crumbed goat cheese salad

Buy cooked beets or, better still, cook your own beforehand, then team with flash-fried crumbed goat cheese for a fast and simple sit-down first course.

Cut the goat cheese into 4 slices, around ½ inch thick. Coat each slice in olive oil, then in the bread crumbs, and chill until required.

Peel the cooked beets by rubbing off the skin. Trim neatly, slice into paper-thin rounds, and arrange in an overlapping ring on each dinner plate. Whisk the dressing ingredients together in a bowl. Toss the arugula or spinach leaves lightly in the dressing and arrange in the center of the beets.

Heat a nonstick frying pan, and dry-fry each slice of goat cheese until golden brown, carefully turning once. Gently lift the goat cheese onto the leaves (it may break up, but that's okay). Drizzle any remaining dressing over and around.

SERVES 4

7oz fresh, firm goat cheese
(in a round or log form)
2 tbsp extra virgin olive oil
3 tbsp fine, dry bread crumbs
4 medium beets, cooked
7oz baby arugula or spinach
leaves (about 2 cups)

Dressing:
2 tbsp extra virgin olive oil
1 tbsp white wine vinegar
1 tbsp finely snipped chives
sea salt
freshly ground black pepper

oatcakes with goat cheese

Gazpacho with cucumber

This isn't so much a cold soup, as a fresh and healthy vegetable smoothie. If you're feeling flash, drop a cooked shrimp into each bowl, as a surprise bonus.

Roughly chop the tomatoes, cucumber, bell peppers, onion, and garlic, and combine in a blender.

Cut off the crusts from the bread and discard. Place the bread in a bowl with just enough water to cover, then immediately squeeze out the water and roughly tear the bread into pieces.

Add the bread to the blender with the sherry vinegar, olive oil, Tabasco, sea salt, and pepper. Whiz for a minute or two, until smooth. Press through a fine sieve into a bowl, then cover and chill until ready to serve.

Place a shrimp (if using) in each chilled cocktail glass or serving bowl, and top with the vegetable gazpacho. Scatter diced bell pepper and cucumber on top.

SERVES 4

6 ripe tomatoes

1 hothouse cucumber, peeled and seeded

2 red bell peppers, cored and seeded

1 small onion, peeled

1 garlic clove, peeled

3 thick slices sourdough bread

2 tbsp sherry vinegar

2 tbsp extra virgin olive oil

dash of Tabasco

sea salt

freshly ground black pepper

To serve:

4 cooked, peeled, large shrimp (optional)

2 tbsp diced red bell pepper

2 tbsp diced cucumber

Oatcakes with goat cheese

Why make them when you can buy them? Because they're so much better homemade. Top with oven-roasted cherry tomatoes and tangy goat cheese, and serve with drinks.

Heat the oven to 350°F. Toss the cherry tomatoes in olive oil and bake for 15 minutes until soft and squidgy. Remove and cool to room temperature.

To make the oatcakes, whiz the oats, flour, butter, and salt in a food processor. Add water, 1 tbsp at a time, until the mixture starts to come together.

Push the dough together with your hands, then gently roll or pat it out on a lightly floured surface until $1/2$ inch thick. Cut into 2-inch rounds with a cookie cutter or upturned liqueur glass. Re-roll the scraps and cut out more rounds.

Place the oatcakes on a nonstick baking sheet and bake for 10 to 12 minutes. Cool on a wire rack and store in an airtight container. Serve topped with a thin slice of goat cheese and a cherry tomato.

MAKES 20
20 cherry tomatoes
1 tbsp extra virgin olive oil
$1\frac{1}{2}$ cups rolled oats
$2/3$ cup all-purpose flour
6 tbsp butter, softened
1 tsp sea salt
2–4 tbsp cold water
7oz fresh, firm goat cheese
(in a round log)

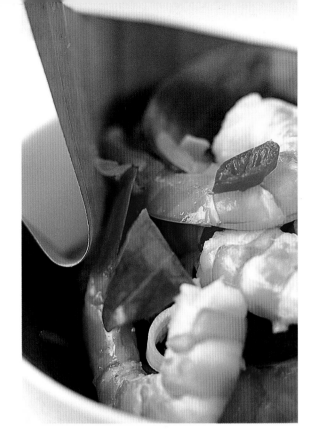

Coconut shrimp with chili

This is fast, simple, and comes with all those tangy tastes you love in Thai food. No time? Then use cooked shrimp and add a little coconut milk to the dressing.

Devein the shrimp by hooking a thin bamboo skewer through the spine and pulling out the black thread, but don't peel them. Heat the coconut milk, salt, and water in a pan until simmering. Add the shrimp and simmer for 3 to 4 minutes until they change color. Remove and cool, then peel, leaving the tail intact.

Trim the lemongrass and finely slice the white section only. Finely slice the chilies and shallots. Cut the kaffir lime leaves (if using) into thin ribbons.

Combine the lemongrass, chilies, shallots, lime leaves or zest, mint, and cilantro in a bowl. Add the shrimp and toss gently. Add the lime juice, fish sauce, and 2 tbsp of the coconut broth, and toss lightly. Serve at room temperature, scattered with crushed peanuts.

SERVES 4
16 medium, raw shrimp
1 cup canned coconut milk
salt
1 cup water
1 lemongrass stem
2 small, hot red chili peppers
4 shallots, peeled
4 kaffir lime leaves, or
1 tsp grated lime zest
handful of mint leaves
handful of cilantro leaves
2 tbsp lime juice
2 tbsp Thai fish sauce
(nam pla)
2 tbsp salted peanuts, crushed

Belgian mussels

Belgians really know how to cook mussels, and how to eat them – by turning the first empty shell into a pair of tongs in order to pick up the remaining mussels from their shells. Serve with crusty bread and a pot of real mayonnaise for dipping.

Scrub the mussels well, pulling out the little beards, and discard any that don't close when tapped.

Peel the onion and slice into fine rings. Heat the butter and oil in a large lidded pan, and cook the onion gently for 5 minutes.

Add the white wine, chicken stock, celery, and garlic cloves, and bring to a boil. Add the mussels, cover with the lid, and cook for 1 minute, then shake the pan, remove the lid, and take out the mussels that have opened.

Repeat this process a few times, discarding any mussels that refuse to open. Add the cream and parsley to the pan, and gently warm through, stirring.

Distribute the mussels among 4 warmed, deep soup bowls and pour the creamy broth on top.

SERVES 4

3lb mussels

1 onion

1 tbsp butter

1 tbsp olive oil

1 cup dry white wine

1 cup light chicken stock or water

2 celery stalks, finely sliced

2 garlic cloves, peeled and smashed

2 tbsp light cream

2 tbsp chopped parsley

simple brunches

Sweet onion crostini

If brunch is half breakfast, half lunch – and better than both – then this sweet, slow-cooked onion with Italian prosciutto on hot toast is perfect brunch material. You can use Spanish jamón serrano if you prefer.

Peel the onions and slice finely into rings. Melt the butter with the oil in a heavy-based frying pan, add the onions, sea salt, pepper, and rosemary, and cook gently for 20 minutes, tossing occasionally, until soft and translucent.

Turn up the heat, add the white wine, and allow it to bubble and reduce, stirring well. Lower the heat and cook for a further 10 to 15 minutes until the onions are soft and gooey. Add the wine vinegar, and toss well. You can leave the onions as they are, which I prefer, or purée them in a food processor and reheat the purée.

Toast the bread on both sides. Pile a generous amount of sweet onions on the toast and top with folded slices of prosciutto. Tuck in the rosemary sprigs and serve.

SERVES 4

4 large white onions

1 tbsp butter

1 tbsp olive oil

sea salt

freshly ground black pepper

2 rosemary sprigs

1 cup white wine

1 tbsp red wine vinegar

4 thick slices sourdough bread

8 thin slices prosciutto

4 rosemary sprigs, to serve

Catalan tomato bread
Cut 4 big, soft buns in half and lightly toast
under the broiler. Brush with olive oil and rub
with a cut garlic clove. Halve 4 ripe tomatoes
and rub over the buns, squeezing the juices
and seeds into the bread. Broil until browned,
and serve with egg dishes, cured meats,
and cheeses.

Amish pancakes

Soft, light, oatmeal pancakes to stack high with crisp bacon or soft prosciutto, and drizzle with maple syrup.

Heat the milk to just below boiling point, remove from the heat, and add the rolled oats and sugar. Stir well, and leave to cool.

Sift the flour, baking powder, and salt together into a large bowl, add the cooled mixture, and stir well. Beat the egg yolks lightly and stir into the mixture.

Beat the egg whites in a dry bowl until stiff and peaky, then lightly fold into the pancake batter.

Broil or pan-fry the bacon slices (if using) until crisp, and drain on paper towel.

Heat a large nonstick frying pan and add a teaspoon of butter. Drop tablespoons of batter into the pan and cook over medium heat. When bubbles appear on top, turn and cook the other side until golden. Remove and keep warm. Add another teaspoon of butter, and repeat to cook the rest of the pancakes.

Serve 2 or 3 pancakes per person. Stack them with bacon or prosciutto and drizzle with maple syrup.

MAKES 12
$1^3/_4$ cups milk
$1^1/_4$ cups rolled oats
1 tbsp sugar
1 tbsp all-purpose flour
2 tsp baking powder
pinch of salt
2 extra-large free-range eggs, separated
8 thin slices bacon or prosciutto
unsalted butter for frying
maple syrup, to serve

Little egg and ham pies

Line each cup of a muffin pan with ham, crack an egg into it, add cream and a little grated cheese, and bake. Serve warm for brunch, or take on a picnic.

Heat the oven to 350°F. Lightly oil or butter a 12-hole muffin pan. Line the bottom and most of the sides of each cup with a slice of ham, then break an egg into the hollow. Drizzle with the cream, and scatter with sea salt, pepper, parsley, and parmesan.

Bake for 15 to 20 minutes until the egg is just set and starting to shrink away from the sides of the cup. Leave to cool for 5 minutes, then run a knife around each cup to loosen the ham and egg, and remove to a wire rack. Eat warm, or at room temperature.

MAKES 12
1 tsp olive oil or butter
12 thin slices good-quality ham
12 extra-large free-range eggs
2 tbsp cream
sea salt
freshly ground black pepper
2 tbsp roughly chopped parsley
4 tbsp freshly grated parmesan

chicken pies

Chicken pies

Buy a ready-roasted chicken or a Chinatown soy chicken, and these simple, warm chicken pies are even simpler.

Heat the oven to 400°F. Soak the dried shiitake mushrooms in hot water to cover for 30 minutes. Strip the meat from the chicken and chop it finely.

Peel and mince the shallots. Drain the mushrooms, trim off the stems, and slice the caps finely.

Heat the oil in a pan, and cook the shallots gently until soft. Sprinkle with the flour and cook, stirring, for 2 minutes. Gradually add the chicken stock, stirring. Add the mushrooms, and soy, oyster, and hoi sin sauces, and simmer for 5 minutes. Remove from the heat, stir in the chicken and cilantro, and leave to cool.

Roll out half the pastry and cut into twelve 5-inch squares. Repeat with the other half. Plop 1 tbsp of the chicken mixture on a pastry square, top with another square, and press down around the filling to seal. Place a large upturned glass over the top, and trim the pie into a circle. Repeat until all pies are made.

Brush the pies with egg yolk, cut a small slash in the top, and bake for 20 to 25 minutes until golden.

MAKES 12

6 dried shiitake mushrooms

1 medium chicken, roasted
   or poached

4 shallots, or 1 small onion

2 tbsp peanut oil

1 tbsp all-purpose flour

1 cup chicken stock

1 tbsp soy sauce

1 tbsp oyster sauce

1 tbsp hoi sin or plum sauce

2 tbsp minced cilantro

1 lb puff pastry

1 egg yolk, beaten with
   1 tbsp milk

Country terrine

A hearty, rustic country pâté to serve with crusty bread, little green cornichons, and salad leaves.

Roughly chop the bacon, reserving the 4 slices for the top. Clean and trim the chicken livers, and roughly chop.

Combine the ground pork, bacon, and chicken livers in a large bowl, along with the minced herbs, shallots, garlic, salt, pepper, nutmeg, and brandy. Mix well with your hands, then cover and leave in the refrigerator overnight.

Heat the oven to 350°F. Mix the egg into the meat and pile the mixture into a 1-quart ovenproof dish. Shape the top into a mound and cover with the reserved bacon. Cover with a tight-fitting lid or foil, and bake for 1$\frac{1}{2}$ hours, or until the pâté starts to shrink away from the sides of the dish. Cool slightly, then drain off some of the fat. Serve at room temperature, topped with thyme sprigs.

SERVES 8

7oz sliced center-cut bacon, plus 4 extra slices

8oz chicken livers

2lb coarsely ground fatty pork

1 tbsp minced parsley

1 tbsp minced thyme

1 tbsp minced sage

2 shallots, peeled and finely sliced

2 garlic cloves, peeled and crushed

2 tsp salt

$\frac{1}{2}$ tsp freshly ground black pepper

$\frac{1}{2}$ tsp freshly grated nutmeg

2 tbsp brandy or port

1 extra-large free-range egg, beaten

thyme sprigs, to serve

Figs and baked ricotta

Place 1 lb (2 cups) fresh ricotta in a baking dish. Scatter with sea salt, pepper, thyme, and rosemary, drizzle with extra virgin olive oil, and bake at 400°F for 15 minutes. Add 6 halved ripe figs and bake for another 10 minutes. Serve with prosciutto, drizzled with olive oil and balsamic vinegar.

Egyptian beet dip

Whiz 5 cooked, peeled beets in a blender with $1\frac{1}{4}$ cups yogurt, 2 crushed garlic cloves, 2 tbsp lemon juice, 2 tbsp extra virgin olive oil, sea salt, pepper, and $\frac{1}{2}$ tsp each of ground cumin, coriander, paprika, and cinnamon. Serve with warm flat bread for dipping.

Two fruity drinks

Icy cold, silky smooth, and highly energizing, a frozen Indian lassi is sheer liquid food. Or, if you have a juice extractor, try the wake-up juice below.

SERVES 4

3 bananas, peeled

1 cup red berries

1 cup plain low-fat yogurt

1 tbsp clear honey

1 cup orange juice

Place the bananas in a plastic bag and freeze for an hour or two until firm. Whiz the bananas, berries, yogurt, honey, and orange juice together in a blender until smooth and creamy.

Adjust the sweetness (add more honey if the berries are tart) and thickness (add more orange juice to thin the drink if needed). Serve the lassi in chilled glasses.

SERVES 4

1 beet

3 green-skinned apples

1/2-inch cube of fresh ginger

Scrub the beet, apples, and ginger clean, and cut them into segments small enough to fit into your juice extractor. Juice the beet first, then the ginger, and finally, the apples, which will help clear the machine of the beet. Dilute the wake-up juice with cold filtered water to taste.

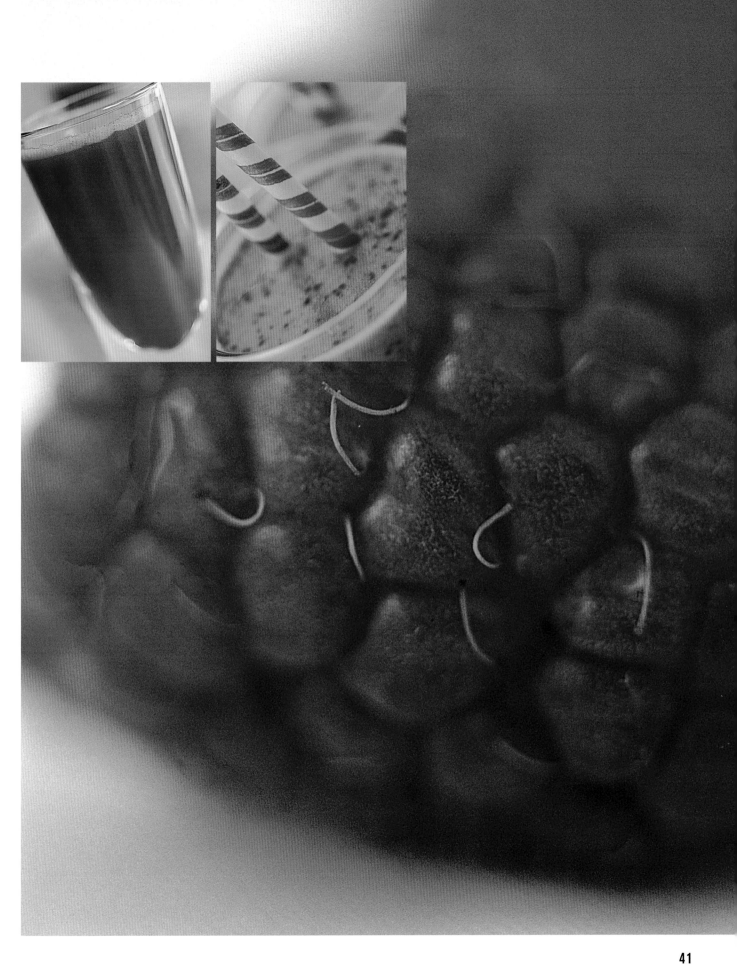

Tunisian salad pitas

One of the world's crunchiest, freshest salads. Serve it with lightly warmed pita bread, or stuff it into the pita pocket and eat in your hands.

Mince the red bell pepper, discarding the core and seeds. Cut the tomatoes in half, squeeze out and discard the seeds and juice, and mince the flesh. Mince the radishes, green onions and hard-boiled eggs. Combine the red pepper, tomatoes, radishes, green onions, eggs, capers, and tuna in a large bowl.

Whisk the lemon juice, olive oil, sea salt, pepper, coriander, and caraway together. Pour this spiced oil over the salad and toss well.

Lightly warm the pita breads in the oven or under the broiler, then cut off the top $1/2$ inch and fill the pita pockets with the salad.

SERVES 4
1 red bell pepper
2 tomatoes
2 small radishes
2 green onions
2 hard-boiled eggs, peeled
1 tbsp tiny capers, rinsed
10 oz canned tuna in oil, drained
8 pita breads

Spiced oil:
2 tsp lemon juice
1 tbsp olive oil
sea salt
freshly ground black pepper
$1/2$ tsp ground coriander
$1/2$ tsp ground caraway

aromatic, cheeky herbs

Variety isn't the spice of life, after all - it's the herb.

Change the herb and you alter the smell, the taste, and the look of

your food. Simple, really.

bite into a fresh herb sandwich
Finely snip a handful of chives and mix with some minced mint, parsley, and thyme. Sandwich between slices of fresh white bread, spread with cream cheese or fresh ricotta spiked with sea salt and black pepper.

add fresh mint to your salad greens
Add a handful of fresh mint leaves to your next green leaf salad, dress it with 2 tbsp extra virgin olive oil, 1 tbsp red wine vinegar, sea salt, pepper, and 1 tsp Dijon mustard, and every mouthful will taste wild.

add fragrance to fruit
Fruits love herbs, not just spices. Add basil to fresh ripe peaches and pineapple. Chop fresh mint and papaya, and toss with a squeeze of lime juice and a little sugar. Poach apricots or plums in a light sugar syrup with bay leaves and peppercorns.

a simple way with sage
Fry sage leaves in olive oil until crisp, then remove. Use the oil to pan-fry mushrooms, potatoes, crumbed veal, pork chops, or duck breasts. Serve topped with the crisp-fried sage leaves.

give the knife a rest
You don't always have to chop fresh herbs. Chives are better snipped with scissors, and basil leaves are better simply torn. Throw whole parsley, sage, and oregano leaves into pasta sauces, soups, and stews, and strew whole sprigs of thyme and rosemary over roasts.

add an herb crust to fish

Mix 2 tbsp chopped basil, parsley, and chervil with 1 cup of soft bread crumbs, salt, pepper, a pinch of cayenne, and a squeeze of lime juice. Dip 4 fish fillets into beaten egg, then into the herb crumbs, and fry until crisp and golden.

marinate everything in sight

Marinate lamb chops with rosemary or oregano in olive oil before broiling. Marinate chicken in cilantro, mint, basil, and vegetable oil before grilling. Marinate sliced tomatoes and goat cheese in thyme, garlic, and olive oil, and serve all summer long.

bay-leaf your meatballs

Make your favorite bite-sized meatballs, wrap a lightly oiled bay leaf around each one, and secure with a wooden toothpick. Bake and serve, but don't eat the leaf.

zap your potato salad

Chives are the obvious pick, but try spiking potato salad with a gremolata – 2 crushed garlic cloves tossed with 2 tbsp minced parsley and 1 tbsp grated lemon rind – and prepare to be amazed. Scatter the same gremolata over pan-fried fish, parmesan risotto, roast chicken, and baked mushrooms.

make a pot of herb tea

Add boiling water to a handful of crushed mint or basil, or a few stems of bashed lemongrass, and leave to steep for 5 minutes. Strain and serve with a sprig of the same herb for a great late-afternoon pick-me-up.

simple lunches

Mediterranean vegetables

A meal in itself for vegetable lovers, or a simple, colorful accompaniment to fish, sausages, lamb, or chicken.

Heat the oven to 350°F. Cut the onion in half and slice finely. Cut the red and yellow bell peppers into long strips, discarding the core and seeds.

Heat the 1 tbsp oil in a frying pan, and fry the onion and peppers for 10 minutes until they start to soften. Slice the zucchini and tomatoes into rings.

Arrange the onion and peppers in the bottom of a lightly oiled baking pan or gratin dish, and layer the sliced zucchini and tomatoes on top – in any order you like.

Mix the extra virgin olive oil with the lemon juice, garlic, rosemary, thyme, sea salt, and pepper. Drizzle over the vegetables and bake for about 1 hour until tender. Serve hot or warm.

SERVES 4

1 onion, peeled

1 red bell pepper

1 yellow bell pepper

1 tbsp olive oil

4 medium zucchini

4 Roma tomatoes

2 tbsp extra virgin olive oil

1 tbsp lemon juice

1 garlic clove, peeled and
    crushed

4 rosemary sprigs

6 thyme sprigs

sea salt

freshly ground black pepper

Couscous with dates

Golden couscous makes a light and healthy lunch, with a spicy, fragrant broth and some simple steamed vegetables.

Heat the oven to 325°F. Place the couscous in a large heatproof bowl and pour the boiling water on top. Add the olive oil and diced butter, and toss them through with a fork. Cover and place in the oven for 15 minutes.

Meanwhile, finely slice the onions. Heat the oil in a pan and fry the onions until soft. Add the garlic, tomatoes, sugar, salt, pepper, saffron, paprika, ginger, and parsley, and simmer for 10 minutes.

Steam or lightly boil the zucchini, dried apricots, and dates for 5 minutes, then drain and thickly slice the zucchini.

Run a fork through the couscous to break up any lumps and season with salt. Pile into warm bowls and top with the zucchini, apricots, and dates. Serve, with the hot tomato broth on the side.

SERVES 4
Couscous:
$2^2/_3$ cups couscous
2 cups boiling water
1 tbsp olive oil
1 tbsp butter, diced

Vegetables and broth:
2 onions, peeled
2 tbsp olive oil
2 garlic cloves, peeled and crushed
16oz canned crushed tomatoes
1 tsp sugar
sea salt
freshly ground black pepper
$^1/_2$ tsp powdered saffron
1 tsp paprika
1 tsp ground ginger
2 tbsp chopped parsley
6 zucchini, green and yellow, or other summer squash
12 dried apricots
10 moist, dried dates, pitted and sliced

Lamb steak sandwich

This is even nicer than the more traditional steak sandwich, as lamb teams with sweetly caramelized onions for a hearty weekend lunch.

Heat the oven to 350°F. Finely slice the onions and toss in a roasting pan with 2 tbsp olive oil, the balsamic vinegar, salt, and pepper. Bake for 30 to 40 minutes until caramelized.

Flatten each lamb steak or tenderloin with a meat mallet, then cut in two. Combine the extra virgin olive oil, white wine, garlic, and oregano in a shallow dish, add the lamb, and coat well.

Slice the tomatoes and season with salt and pepper. Beat the mustard into the mayonnaise.

Lightly oil a nonstick frying pan and heat. When it is very hot, add the lamb and sear until crusty, turning once. This will only take a minute or two either side. Season well, and set aside while you toast the bread.

Spread 4 toast slices with the mustard mayonnaise, and arrange the arugula leaves, tomatoes, lamb, and caramelized onions on top. Top with the remaining toast slices.

SERVES 4

3 white onions

2 tbsp olive oil

2 tbsp balsamic vinegar

sea salt

freshly ground black pepper

4 boneless lamb leg steaks or
tenderloin, around 6oz each

2 tbsp extra virgin olive oil

2 tbsp white wine

1 garlic clove, smashed

1 tbsp oregano leaves

4 vine-ripened tomatoes

1 tbsp Dijon mustard

1 cup good mayonnaise

8 thick slices sourdough or
light rye bread

7oz baby arugula leaves
(about 2 cups)

Haloumi, tomato, and beans

Fresh haloumi is a rich, salty, Greek-Cypriot cheese sold pre-packed in plastic, with a little brine.

Heat the oven to 350°F. Cut the tomatoes in half lengthwise and arrange in a baking pan. Drizzle with 1 tbsp olive oil, sea salt, pepper, and thyme, and bake for 30 minutes until soft.

Cook the green beans in simmering salted water for 5 minutes.

Rinse the haloumi, then cut into slices a little less than ½ inch thick. Heat the remaining olive oil in a nonstick frying pan and, when hot, sizzle the haloumi slices until golden brown. Turn briefly and sizzle the other side.

Whisk the lemon juice, olive oil, capers, and parsley together. Drain the beans and toss in the dressing. Arrange the tomatoes and beans on 4 dinner plates, and top with haloumi. Drizzle with the dressing and serve, with lemon.

SERVES 4

8 plum tomatoes
2 tbsp olive oil
sea salt
freshly ground black pepper
few thyme sprigs
14 oz green beans, trimmed
14 oz haloumi
1 lemon, quartered

Dressing:
1 tbsp lemon juice
2 tbsp extra virgin olive oil
1 tbsp capers, rinsed
1 tbsp chopped parsley

sizzle haloumi until golden

French café salad

You can make a different café salad every day – from eggs, potatoes, and tuna, or chicken, beans, and tomato, or asparagus, avocado, and ham – you get the idea.

Heat the oven to 400°F. Cut the tomatoes in half and arrange in a baking pan. Season with sea salt and pepper, drizzle with 1 tbsp olive oil, and bake for 20 minutes.

Cook the potatoes and beans in simmering salted water until tender. Drain and cut the potatoes in half. Peel the hard-boiled eggs and cut into quarters.

Heat 1 tbsp olive oil in a nonstick frying pan and sear the tuna steaks for 3 minutes on each side, leaving the inside pink.

To make the dressing, in a large bowl whisk the wine vinegar, olive oil, and mustard with sea salt and pepper until thick.

Dress the arugula leaves, potatoes, beans, and olives, and arrange on dinner plates with the tomatoes and eggs. Cut the tuna into chunks and place on top, with the anchovy fillets.

SERVES 4
4 plum tomatoes
sea salt
freshly ground black pepper
2 tbsp olive oil
8 small potatoes, peeled
8oz fine green beans, trimmed
4 hard-boiled eggs
2 fresh tuna steaks, around 10oz each, trimmed
7oz arugula or spinach leaves (about 2 cups)
2 tbsp small black olives
4 anchovy fillets, halved

Dressing:
2 tbsp red wine vinegar
4 tbsp extra virgin olive oil
1 tsp Dijon mustard

beet burgers

spanish meatballs

Beet burgers

Australians love beets with their burgers, but this idea is actually from Sweden, where beets are added to the meat to give it a sweet tang.

Mince the onion. Heat the butter and olive oil in a frying pan, and cook the onion slowly until pale and soft, then cool.

Combine the ground beef, egg yolks, capers, sea salt, and pepper in a bowl, add the onion, and mix together thoroughly. Add the pickled beets and juice, and mix well. With wet hands, shape the mixture into 4 large, flat burgers (the traditional method) or make 8 smaller, taller patties.

Heat a ridged cast-iron grill pan, oil it and the burgers lightly, and cook them on a medium heat for about 5 minutes each side. (Alternatively heat a little olive oil in a frying pan and cook the burgers over medium heat until brown on each side.)

Meanwhile, toast the muffins. Serve the burgers in the toasted muffins, with a little salad of green leaves, or with wilted spinach and small boiled potatoes.

SERVES 4

1 onion, peeled

1 tbsp butter

1 tbsp olive oil

1lb ground beef

2 egg yolks

1 tbsp capers, rinsed and
   chopped

sea salt

freshly ground black pepper

3 tbsp minced pickled beets

1 tbsp pickled beet juice

4 English muffins

Spanish meatballs

Do this ahead of time and serve as a lazy, light lunch with some salad, and the Catalan tomato bread on page 29.

Trim off the crusts and soak the bread in the milk for 5 minutes, then squeeze dry. Using your hands, mix the bread with the meat, garlic, nutmeg, parsley, egg, salt, and pepper. Form the mixture into small balls the size of a walnut, and roll in the flour.

Chop the onion. Cut the green bell pepper into strips, discarding the seeds.

Heat the olive oil in a heavy-based frying pan, and cook the meatballs in batches until well browned on all sides. Remove and add a little extra oil to the pan. Add the onion and green pepper and cook, stirring, for 5 minutes.

Return the meatballs to the pan, and add the crushed tomatoes, green olives, salt, pepper, sherry, and stock. Bring to a boil, then simmer for 30 to 45 minutes until the sauce has reduced and thickened to a sludge. Serve hot.

MAKES 30
2 thick slices stale bread
½ cup milk
1 lb ground lamb or beef
1 garlic clove, peeled
and crushed
½ tsp freshly grated nutmeg
1 tbsp minced parsley
1 free-range egg
sea salt
freshly ground black pepper
2 tbsp all-purpose flour
1 onion, peeled
½ green bell pepper
2 tbsp olive oil
28 oz canned crushed tomatoes
12 green Spanish olives
3 tbsp dry sherry
1 cup chicken stock

Honey-soy quail

Although it is baked in the oven, this crisp-skinned quail tastes as if it has been barbecued over hot coals in Chinatown, which is exactly how you want it to taste.

Wash the quail and pat dry. Tuck the wing tips in behind the body, and tie the legs together with string. Mix the honey and soy sauce in a bowl, add the quail, and coat well. Leave to marinate for 30 minutes. Mix the five-spice powder with the salt and set aside.

Heat the oven to 400°F. Drain the quail, place in a baking pan, and drizzle with the sesame oil. Bake the quail for 30 minutes, turning them around once or twice, until the meat is cooked and the skin is crisp and browned.

Serve on a bed of wilted green onions or spinach, or with the sesame snow peas on page 78. Sprinkle with the five-spiced salt and serve with sweet chili sauce.

SERVES 4

4 fresh quail, around
7oz each
2 tbsp clear honey
3 tbsp soy sauce
1 tsp five-spice powder
1 tsp salt
1 tsp toasted sesame oil
2 tbsp sweet, seedy Thai
chili sauce

Parmesan lamb chops

I've always loved crumbed lamb chops, either hot with mashed potato and peas, or cold on a picnic with a spicy tomato relish. These chops have a cheese crumb that makes them even nicer.

Flatten the meat with a meat mallet, leaving it on the bone. Put the flour, salt, and pepper in a plastic bag, and toss each chop in the flour, shaking off any excess.

Place the eggs in a shallow bowl, and mix the parmesan and bread crumbs together in another one.

Heat the oil and butter in a large, heavy-based frying pan. Dip each chop in the beaten egg, then in the parmesan crumbs to coat, and fry over medium heat on both sides until crisp and golden brown.

Drain the crumbed chops on paper towel. Serve with lemon, and a sharply dressed green salad.

SERVES 4

12 lamb rib chops, well
   trimmed
2 tbsp all-purpose flour
sea salt
freshly ground black pepper
2 free-range eggs, beaten
2 tbsp finely grated parmesan
4 tbsp dry bread crumbs
2 tbsp light olive oil
1 tbsp butter
1 lemon, quartered

Mixed grill

When I was growing up in Australia, a mixed grill was the best pub lunch around. This is a bit classier, but just as good.

Cut the tenderloin into 4 pieces. Prick the sausages, and cut bacon slices in half. Heat a ridged cast-iron grill pan or charcoal grill.

Cut the zucchini on the diagonal into ½-inch slices. Cut the tomatoes in half lengthwise. Brush the zucchini and tomatoes with olive oil and grill until soft.

Brush the sausages with olive oil and grill until browned. Fry the bacon in a nonstick frying pan until crisp. Brush the steaks with olive oil and grill for around 3 minutes on one side, then 1 minute on the other, depending on thickness.

Wash the spinach and shake dry. Whisk the olive oil, vinegar, mustard, sea salt, and pepper together until thick, dress the leaves, and arrange on plates. Top with the grilled vegetables and meats.

SERVES 4

10 oz beef tenderloin or
4 filet mignon steaks
12 small, spicy, fresh beef
sausages (chipolatas)
4 thin slices bacon
2 zucchini
4 plum tomatoes
1 tbsp olive oil
3½ oz baby spinach leaves
(about 1 cup)

Dressing:
2 tbsp extra virgin olive oil
1 tbsp red wine vinegar
1 tsp Dijon mustard
sea salt
freshly ground black pepper

simple salads

Yellow pepper salad

Put these warm, sunny flavors with sliced prosciutto and fresh crusty bread for a lazy lunch, or with grilled fish, chicken, or lamb at any time.

Heat the oven to 400°F. Place the bell peppers in a baking pan and coat with a little of the olive oil. Bake for 20 minutes, turning once or twice, until lightly scorched. Alternatively you can grill the oiled peppers on a cast-iron grill pan, or broil them.

Remove peppers from the heat and place in a bowl. Cover and leave for 10 minutes, then peel away the skin, and remove the core and seeds. Cut the flesh lengthwise into thick strips.

Arrange the pepper strips on a serving plate. Combine the olives, remaining olive oil, sea salt, and pepper, and drizzle over the top. Scatter with basil leaves or sprigs of thyme.

SERVES 4

2 yellow and 2 orange bell
   peppers (or 4 yellow ones)
2 tbsp extra virgin olive oil
2 tbsp small black olives
sea salt
freshly ground black pepper
few basil leaves, or thyme
   sprigs

Grilled zucchini salad

Slice 6 zucchini lengthwise, brush with olive oil, and grill
or broil. Whisk together 2 tbsp each
lemon juice, extra virgin olive oil,
and chopped dill. Season and
pour over the zucchini.
Serve topped with
grilled lemon.

toss with dill, parsley, or chives

Warm potatoes and capers

Cold potatoes are an abomination, but something quite special happens when warm potatoes hit a generous, mustardy dressing. Eat warm, obviously.

Cook the potatoes in simmering, salted water until tender but still firm, about 20 minutes. Mince the green onions.

In the meantime, make the dressing. Combine the olive oil, wine vinegar, mustard, sea salt, and pepper in a large bowl and whisk well until thickened. Add the capers, green onions, and minced herbs, and toss lightly.

Drain the potatoes and slice them thickly, as soon as you can handle them. Toss them carefully in the dressing, making sure the slices don't stick together. Arrange on warmed plates, drizzle with any extra dressing, and serve.

SERVES 4
6 medium waxy potatoes,
peeled
3 green onions
1 tbsp small capers, rinsed
2 tbsp minced dill, parsley,
or chives

Dressing:
3 tbsp extra virgin olive oil
2 tbsp red wine vinegar
1 tsp Dijon mustard
sea salt
freshly ground black pepper

Chorizo and sweet potato

Cut 2 cooked sweet potatoes and
4 air-dried chorizo sausages thickly
on the diagonal, brush with oil,
and pan-grill until sizzling.
Whisk 1 tbsp lemon juice and
2 tbsp olive oil with 1 tbsp
chopped parsley, then
toss with 7 oz arugula leaves
(about 2 cups). Pile the sizzling
sweet potatoes and sausages on top.

Fattoush

This crunchy Syrian salad combines crisp, toasted bread with fresh, juicy, summery flavors. It's startlingly good with shrimp, lobster, or crab.

Heat the broiler. Open up the flat bread until you have two rounds, and toast under the broiler until crisp and golden. Crumble into small shards with your hands, and set aside.

Peel the cucumbers, cut in half lengthwise, and scoop out and discard the seeds. Halve the tomatoes and scoop out the seeds and juice. Chop the cucumbers, tomatoes, bell pepper, radishes, and green onions, and mix with the parsley and mint.

Whisk the olive oil, lemon juice, cinnamon, sea salt, and pepper together. Toss the salad in the dressing, add the crisp bread, and toss again. Using a slotted spoon, divide the salad among 4 individual plates, or pile onto one big platter.

SERVES 4

1 round of Lebanese flat bread,
   or 2 pita breads
2 small Lebanese or regular
   cucumbers
2 ripe tomatoes
1/2 red bell pepper
4 small radishes
6 green onions
3 tbsp minced parsley
3 tbsp minced mint

Dressing:
4 tbsp olive oil
3 tbsp lemon juice
1/2 tsp ground cinnamon
sea salt
freshly ground black pepper

parsley and lemon salad

Sesame snow peas

Snow peas are too boring for words when cooked whole. But shred them finely and toss them raw in a sweet Asian vinaigrette, and they taste wild. Serve as a salad or side dish, or use as a base for seafood, duck, or grilled quail.

Wash and dry the snow peas, then finely slice lengthwise into matchsticks, using the tip of a sharp knife. This will take some time, but keep going and don't curse me too much. The effect it has on the flavor and texture is too great to give up now.

For the dressing, mix the sugar, soy sauce, wine vinegar, rice wine, and sesame oil together. Lightly toss the shredded snow peas in the dressing, draining off any excess.

Arrange the dressed snow peas on a serving plate and sprinkle with the sesame seeds to serve.

SERVES 4

8oz snow peas (about
   1$\frac{1}{2}$ cups)
2 tsp sesame seeds

Dressing:
1 tsp sugar
1 tbsp soy sauce
1 tbsp rice wine vinegar, or
   white wine vinegar
1 tbsp Chinese rice wine, or
   dry sherry
2 tsp toasted sesame oil

Parsley and lemon salad

The freshest, brightest, herbiest, tangiest salad around, traditionally eaten wrapped in fresh, unsprayed, vine leaves. It's never as good as when you first make it, so eat soon after.

Rinse the bulgur wheat, then soak in cold water to cover for 1 hour, or until swollen.

Chop the green onions. Peel the cucumber, halve, scoop out the seeds, and mince the flesh. Cut the tomatoes in half, squeeze out and discard the seeds and juice, and dice the flesh.

Pick off the herb leaves, wash and dry well, then roughly chop. Drain the bulgur and squeeze dry. Toss with the herbs, green onions, cucumber, and tomato.

Mix the olive oil with the lemon juice, cumin, cayenne, and sea salt. Pour the dressing over the salad, toss well, and serve.

SERVES 4
1 cup fine bulgur wheat
2 green onions
1 small hothouse cucumber
2 tomatoes
2 bunches of parsley
1 bunch of mint

Dressing:
2 tbsp extra virgin olive oil
2 tbsp lemon juice
$\frac{1}{2}$ tsp ground cumin
$\frac{1}{2}$ tsp cayenne pepper
1 tsp sea salt

Chicken Caesar

It's the most popular thing on the café menu, but we can do it better at home. Note this dressing contains raw egg yolk.

To make the dressing, whiz the egg yolk, garlic, anchovy fillets, mustard, wine vinegar, white wine, salt, and pepper in a blender until smooth. With the motor running, gradually add the olive oil.

Heat the broiler. Brush the chicken with olive oil and broil gently for 15 minutes, turning once, or until cooked through. Season the chicken with salt and pepper, and slice thickly. Broil or fry the bacon until crisp, then crumble into shards.

Toast the bread under the broiler, then brush with a little olive oil and cut into cubes to make croûtons. Remove the outer leaves from the lettuce.

Combine the inner lettuce leaves with the croûtons, chicken, and half the dressing in a large bowl. Toss gently, then arrange on serving plates. Scatter with the bacon and parmesan, and drizzle with the remaining dressing.

SERVES 4

3 skinless, boneless chicken
  breast halves

1–2 tbsp extra virgin olive oil

4 slices bacon

2 thick slices sourdough bread

2 heads romaine lettuce

1 tbsp freshly grated parmesan

Dressing:

1 egg yolk

2 garlic cloves, peeled

2 anchovy fillets

1 tsp Dijon mustard

2 tbsp white wine vinegar

1 tbsp white wine

sea salt

freshly ground black pepper

1/2 cup light olive oil

Asian duck salad

Buy half a Chinese roast duck in Chinatown or use leftover roast duck, and turn it into a light, fresh, crunchy salad with a delicate, sweet dressing. Also good with barbecued chicken.

Slice or shred the duck meat, discarding the bones. Cut the carrots into short lengths, then into matchsticks. Slice the snow peas, bell pepper, and scallions lengthwise into matchsticks.

Put the carrots, bell pepper, and bean sprouts in a bowl, pour boiling water over them, then drain and refresh under cold running water. Drain again.

To make the dressing, whisk the mirin, rice vinegar, fish sauce, sugar, salt, pepper, and olive oil together in a bowl.

Add the vegetables and duck to the dressing and toss gently. Pile onto plates and serve, with or without steamed rice.

SERVES 4
½ Chinese roast duck, or
leftover roast duck
2 carrots, peeled
7oz snow peas (about
1⅓ cups)
1 red or yellow bell pepper,
cored and seeded
2 scallions, trimmed
7oz bean sprouts
(about 2 cups)

Dressing:
1 tbsp mirin (Japanese
sweet rice wine)
2 tbsp Japanese rice vinegar
1 tbsp fish sauce
1 tsp sugar
sea salt
freshly ground black pepper
3 tbsp olive oil

juicy, fruity tomatoes

Smash them, sizzle them, slice them, or eat them out of your hand.

Tomatoes add instant flavor, acidity, juicy bits,

and film star color.

buy the perfect tomato
Buy tomatoes that are good enough to eat in your hands: taut-skinned, green-stemmed, perfumed, ripened on the vine before picking, and brought to the market with stems intact, which helps them last longer.

how to peel and seed
Cut out the core, and cut a small cross in the base. Drop the tomatoes into a pot of simmering water for 20 seconds, then remove, run under cold water, and slip off the skins. Cut in half, then squeeze out and discard the seeds and the juice.

instant tomato sauce
Sizzle a basket of whole cherry tomatoes with a spoonful of olive oil in a hot nonstick frying pan until the skins burst, then tip over green beans or asparagus, broiled fish, or pan-fried chicken breast – instant sauce.

simple tomato vinaigrette
Peel, seed, and dice 2 tomatoes, and stir gently with 4 tbsp extra virgin olive oil and 1 tbsp red wine vinegar, plus sea salt and pepper. Spoon over broiled sea bass, or pan-fried salmon.

soft and juicy semi-dried tomatoes
Cut 2¼ lb plum tomatoes lengthwise into three. Place on a rack over a baking pan, sprinkle with sea salt and thyme, and bake at the lowest oven setting overnight until semi-dried. Cool, layer in a sterilized jar, top with olive oil, seal, and keep refrigerated.

intensify the flavor

Baking reduces water content, and concentrates flavor and acidity. Just cut tomatoes in half, drizzle with olive oil, scatter with sea salt and pepper, and bake at 350°F for 30 to 40 minutes or until they smell interesting.

hot and cold pasta sauce

Peel, seed, and roughly chop 4 ripe, red tomatoes and douse in extra virgin olive oil with a few smashed garlic cloves and a handful of basil leaves. Leave for a few hours to intensify, then toss it all through hot linguine.

fast tomato tart

Roll out puff pastry, cut into saucer shapes, brush with egg, prick, and bake at 425°F for 5 minutes. Cover each tart with halved cherry tomatoes tossed in olive oil, basil, sea salt, and pepper, and bake for 15 minutes until golden.

the 10-minute trick

Add a handful of cherry tomatoes to the last 10 minutes of cooking just about anything – parmesan risotto, Spanish rice, roast leg of lamb – they will turn ruby red, soft, and juicy.

easy tomato jam

Seed and chop 2¼ lb tomatoes. Gently simmer for 1 hour with 3 tbsp light brown sugar, 1 tbsp mustard seeds, 2 tbsp red wine vinegar, and 3 tbsp olive oil, until thick and jammy. Season and cool, then store in airtight jars in the fridge.

simple dinners

Roast pesto chicken

This is a good trick: stuff pesto and bread crumbs under the skin to protect the chicken breast from drying out, and you also infuse it with warm, peppery basil.

Heat the oven to 400°F. Wash the chicken breasts and pat dry. Combine the pesto and bread crumbs in a small bowl to make a thick paste, adding a little olive oil if it's too dry.

Work your fingers in between the skin and meat to create a space, leaving the skin attached at one end or along one side. Stuff the pesto mixture under the skin to cover the breast, carefully draw the skin back over it, and reshape.

Heat a nonstick frying pan, add 1 tbsp oil, and sear the chicken skin for a minute or two until lightly golden, then place the chicken skin-side up in a baking pan and drizzle with the remaining olive oil, lemon juice, sea salt, and pepper.

Bake for about 20 minutes, depending on size, until cooked through. Rest for 5 minutes before serving, with an arugula or watercress salad.

SERVES 4

4 chicken breast halves with
   skin, around 7oz each

2 tbsp pesto

2 tbsp fine dry bread crumbs

2 tbsp extra virgin olive oil

1 tbsp lemon juice

sea salt

freshly ground black pepper

Chicken tikka

Yes, you can make Punjabi-style chicken tikka without investing in a tandoor oven. For the best flavor, use leg or thigh rather than breast meat.

Cut the meat into cubes about 2 inches square. Combine the yogurt, lemon juice, garlic, ginger, spices, salt, and vegetable oil in a non-reactive bowl, and mix well. Add the chicken, toss well, and leave to marinate for 2 to 3 hours.

Heat the broiler. Skewer the chicken pieces loosely on thin bamboo skewers, and place on a lightly oiled broiler rack. Broil the chicken, about 6 inches from the heat, for about 5 minutes on each side, until nicely scorched and cooked through. (Alternatively you can place the rack over a baking pan and bake in a preheated oven at 450°F for 10 to 12 minutes.)

Scatter with cilantro or parsley, and serve the chicken tikka with lemon wedges and basmati rice.

SERVES 4
1 lb boneless chicken meat
$^2/_3$ cup plain yogurt
2 tbsp lemon juice
2 garlic cloves, peeled and crushed
1 tbsp finely grated fresh ginger
2 tsp garam masala
$^1/_2$ tsp ground cumin
1 tsp paprika
$^1/_2$ tsp cayenne powder
1 tsp salt
2 tbsp vegetable oil
handful of cilantro or parsley
lemon wedges, to serve

Pork with apple and sage

Top a seared pork chop with a juicy baked apple, and you have an instant fresh apple sauce on the plate.

Heat the oven to 350°F. Mince the onion. Mash 1 tbsp butter with the minced onion, sugar, and 4 sage leaves. Core the apples from the bottom, leaving the stem intact at the top. Fill each hollow with the stuffing.

Stand the apples in a small baking pan, add the white wine, then pour in enough boiling water to come halfway up the side of the apples. Bake for 45 minutes, or until soft and squishy.

Heat the olive oil and remaining 1 tbsp butter in a heavy-based frying pan with 4 sage leaves. Add the pork chops and cook over medium heat for around 8 to 10 minutes. Season well with sea salt and pepper. Turn the chops and cook for another 5 minutes or until tender.

Place the pork chops on warmed plates, top with the baked apples, and tuck in the remaining sage leaves. Serve with mash.

SERVES 4

½ onion, peeled

2 tbsp butter

1 tbsp sugar

12 sage leaves

4 crisp, tart apples
   (eg Granny Smith)

1 cup dry white wine

1 tbsp olive oil

4 thick pork loin chops

sea salt

freshly ground black pepper

instant apple sauce

Beef sukiyaki

This isn't the traditional cook-at-the-table dish, but a quick dinner of beef and cellophane noodles. These thin, dried, white noodles are made from mung bean flour – you will find them in Asian food stores.

Pour boiling water over the noodles to cover them and let stand for 3 minutes. Cut the tofu into cubes. Mince the green onions and white onion. Slice the beef as finely as you can.

In a small pan, combine the water and dashi powder, then add the soy sauce, mirin, and sugar, and heat gently, stirring. Rinse the soaked noodles in cold water, drain, and set aside.

Heat half the oil in a heavy-based frying pan, and cook all the onions until soft. Add the noodles, tofu, spinach, and dashi sauce, bring to a boil, and simmer for 2 to 3 minutes.

Heat the remaining oil in a second frying pan until hot, and sear the beef slices for a few seconds until just cooked but still pink. Divide the noodle mixture among warmed bowls or plates and top with the seared beef. Serve with rice.

SERVES 4

7oz cellophane or mung bean noodles

7oz fresh tofu

4 green onions

1 white onion, peeled

14oz beef tenderloin or filet

$\frac{1}{2}$ cup water

1 tbsp instant dashi powder

3 tbsp soy sauce

3 tbsp mirin (Japanese sweet rice wine)

1 tbsp sugar

2 tbsp peanut oil

7oz spinach leaves (about 2 cups), well rinsed

eggplant and lamb

Eggplant and lamb

Lamb steaks are much more interesting if they are bashed flat and quickly seared, leaving them nice and juicy inside.

Flatten the lamb with a meat mallet. Mix 2 tbsp olive oil with the lemon juice, rosemary, and thyme, and use to coat the lamb.

Heat the broiler. Slice each eggplant lengthwise into 8 flat, $\frac{1}{2}$-inch-thick slices. Brush with olive oil, season with salt and pepper, and broil on both sides until scorched and tender.

Meanwhile, remove spinach stems and wash the leaves well. Stuff the wet leaves into a saucepan and cook gently, covered, without any extra water, for a few minutes until wilted. Drain and keep warm.

Heat a heavy-based frying pan, or ridged cast-iron grill pan, until hot. Cook the lamb for 2 minutes on either side. Season well, and rest on a warm plate.

Gently squeeze the spinach dry, and toss with a little olive oil, salt, and pepper. Place an eggplant slice on each warmed plate. Top with spinach, more eggplant, then lamb, and finally spinach. Spoon the pesto on top and serve.

SERVES 4

4 boneless lamb leg steaks or
   tenderloin, around 7oz each
3–4 tbsp extra virgin olive oil
1 tbsp lemon juice
3 rosemary sprigs
10 thyme sprigs
2 large eggplants
sea salt
freshly ground black pepper
2lb spinach (not baby)
2 tbsp pesto

Crash hot potatoes

This is one of those crazy little recipes that, once tried, is immediately incorporated into your own repertoire. It's what you want when you want a crisp, roast potato, only better. And all you have to do is boil some small potatoes, smash them flat, and blast them in a hot oven until they are terminally crisp. Serve with eggplant and lamb (see left), pan-fried fish, broiled sausages, or even on their own, with drinks.

Heat the oven to 500°F or the highest setting. Don't peel the potatoes. Just bung them into a pot of salted water, bring to a boil, and simmer for around 15 minutes, until they'll take a skewer without too much resistance. They should be just about cooked, without being soft.

Drain the potatoes and arrange on a lightly oiled baking pan. Use a potato masher to squash each potato flat, until it is twice its original diameter. Brush the tops with olive oil, and scatter with sea salt, black pepper, fennel seeds, and thyme sprigs.

Bake the potatoes on the top shelf of the oven for 20 to 25 minutes until crisp and golden. Serve hot.

SERVES 4
16 small, round potatoes
salt
1 tbsp extra virgin olive oil
1 tsp sea salt
freshly ground black pepper
1 tbsp fennel or caraway seeds
small handful of thyme sprigs

Beet rice

Whiz 3 cooked, peeled beets in a blender with sea salt and pepper. Heat a little butter in a frying pan and cook a minced onion until soft. Add 1½ cups arborio rice and stir well. Add ⅔ cup dry white wine, bubble it away, then add 1 quart hot chicken stock. Stir well, cover tightly, and simmer gently for 15 minutes. Add the beet purée and cook for a few more minutes until the rice is tender. Add 2 tbsp freshly grated parmesan and serve.

Caramel salmon and lime

An unbeatable combination of Thai tastes – chili, cilantro, mint, sugar, lime juice, and fish sauce – is just the thing for delicate, rich, pink-flesh salmon.

To make the sauce, dissolve the sugar in the water in a small pan and bring to a boil, stirring. Add the chili, ginger, and garlic, and let it bubble away to reduce (but not boil over) for 4 to 5 minutes until quite syrupy. Remove from the heat, and add the fish sauce and lime juice.

Cut the salmon into bite-sized pieces, about $3/4$ inch square, and coat lightly in the caramel sauce.

Pour boiling water over the bean sprouts, then drain and set aside.

Heat the oil in a nonstick frying pan, and fry the salmon quickly until caramelized, keeping the inside pink.

Combine the salmon, mint, cilantro, green onion, and bean sprouts in a bowl, and toss well. Arrange on warmed dinner plates, spoon the warm sauce over the top, and scatter with peanuts. Serve with lime quarters and plenty of rice.

SERVES 4

4 thick salmon fillets, around
   6oz each
7oz bean sprouts (about
   2 cups)
2 tbsp vegetable oil
1 cup mint leaves
$1/2$ cup cilantro leaves
1 green onion, finely sliced
2 tbsp salted peanuts, crushed
1 lime, quartered

Sauce:
$1/2$ cup packed soft brown
   sugar
$1/2$ cup water
1 hot red chili pepper, finely
   sliced
2-inch piece of fresh
   ginger, finely sliced
2 garlic cloves, peeled and
   smashed
4 tbsp Thai fish sauce
4 tbsp lime juice

fast roast fish

Chinese ginger fish

A quick, easy meal for everyone who loves Cantonese-style steamed fish. The fish is best with the skin left on, as the final hot dressing will cause it to sizzle and crisp, but if you don't like the skin, you can peel it off before steaming.

Peel the ginger and cut into tiny matchsticks. Finely slice the chili and green onions. Gently wash the fish, pat dry, and arrange on a heatproof platter that will fit into your steamer.

Mix the soy, sesame oil, rice wine, and sugar together, and pour over the fish, skin-side up. Scatter the ginger, chili and half the green onions on top, and steam for 8 to 10 minutes, until the flesh parts easily when pierced with a knife.

Transfer the fish to warmed dinner plates and strain the juices over the top. Heat the oil in a small pan until it just starts to smoke, then pour it over the fish. Scatter with the remaining green onions and cilantro, and serve with jasmine rice.

SERVES 4

2-inch piece of fresh
   ginger

1 small hot red chili pepper

3 green onions

4 thick white fish fillets
   with skin (eg haddock or
   cod), around 6 oz each

3 tbsp soy sauce

1 tbsp toasted sesame oil

2 tbsp Chinese rice wine, or
   dry sherry

1 tbsp sugar

4 tbsp peanut oil

3 tbsp cilantro leaves

Fast roast fish

A fabulous way with fish that gives you moist, juicy, good-looking fillets in 10 minutes flat. Buy the fattest, freshest fillets you can find.

Place a baking pan in the oven and heat the oven to 500°F or its highest setting. The pan may buckle slightly in the heat, but carry on regardless.

In the meantime, gently wash the fish and pat dry. Combine the olive oil, parsley, sea salt, and pepper in a bowl, and coat each fish fillet well in the mixture. Cut the lemon into 4 thick slices.

When very hot, remove the pan from the oven, and place the fish on its hot surface. Add the lemon slices, return to the top shelf of the oven, and bake for 10 minutes. If you could only find thin fillets, test after 5 or 6 minutes.

Gently lift each fish fillet onto a warm dinner plate. Top with a warm slice of lemon, letting its juices run over the fish, and serve.

SERVES 4
4 thick white fish fillets (eg cod, haddock, hake), around 7oz each
2 tbsp extra virgin olive oil
1 tbsp minced parsley
sea salt
freshly ground pepper
1 lemon

sweet, sweet onions

Everything good starts with an onion. It gives a base of sweet complexity, a bed for all the other flavors to lie on.

know your onions

Shallots are little red or brown onions with a milder, sweeter flavor – good for salads and fast-cooked dishes. They're easier to peel if you drop them in a pot of boiling water for 3 minutes first. Torpedo shallots are also milder – peel, cut into rings, and lightly fry. The rest you know.

the onion-balsamic trick

For rich, sweet, and fast caramelized onions, heat 1 tbsp butter and 1 tbsp olive oil in a pan. When hot, fry 2 finely sliced onions for 10 minutes, tossing. Add 2 tbsp balsamic vinegar and cook for 5 minutes until crisp, but don't burn.

fast french onion soup

Fry 6 sliced white onions in 2 tbsp butter. Add 1 tbsp flour and cook for 1 to 2 minutes, then add 5 cups beef or chicken stock and simmer for 20 minutes. Top with toasted slices of sourdough bread, scatter with 3 tbsp grated gruyère cheese, and place under the broiler until the cheese bubbles.

one for the boys

Toss 3 finely sliced red onions in 2 tbsp olive oil and place in a baking pan. Top with 4 thick sliced plum tomatoes, and scatter with salt, pepper, thyme, and rosemary. Lay 8 well-pricked, fresh pork or beef sausages on top. Bake at 400°F for 1 hour.

don't cry, baby

To cure onion tears, place onions in the freezer for 10 minutes before cutting, or chop them in the food processor.

sweet and sour onions

Gently simmer 30 small white onions with 2 tbsp tomato paste, ½ cup red wine vinegar, 2 tbsp olive oil, 2 tbsp sugar, 1 bay leaf, 1 cup dry white wine, 1 cup water, and ⅔ cup raisins for 1 hour until tender. Serve with cold meats.

the nicest way to cook onions

Heat 1 tbsp butter, 2 tbsp olive oil, sea salt, 2 bay leaves, ½ cup dry white wine, and 4 finely sliced onions in a pan. Cook very slowly for 45 minutes until meltingly soft. Serve as a sauce, to a roast leg of lamb or pork. Bliss.

how to roast onions

Don't peel, just cut them crosswise through the top as if quartering, but only halfway down. Drizzle with olive oil, scatter with thyme sprigs, and bake at 350°F for 1 hour for soft, sweet, irresistible onions.

the 15-minute dinner

Fry 2 chopped onions in a little butter and oil for 5 minutes. Add some chopped, leftover cooked ham, chicken, or vegetables, and fry for 5 minutes. Stir in 3 eggs, salt, pepper, and a pinch of cayenne, and cook until golden.

everyone loves onion rings

For crisp onion rings, submerge thickly sliced white onion rings in icy cold water for 1 hour. Drain and pat dry with paper towel, toss in flour, and deep-fry. Serve with broiled fish, sausages, steaks, and char-grilled vegetables.

simple
entertaining

Chili-orange duck

Here is a nice twist on duck à l'orange – aromatic, crisp-skinned duck in a sticky, sweet, and spicy citrus syrup that glows on the plate.

Scrub the oranges well. Cut the rind from 2 oranges, using a sharp knife, and trim off most of the pith. Cut the rind into short, thin strips. Squeeze the juice from the oranges – you need 1 cup.

Combine the orange rind and juice, sugar, ginger, chili, star anise, cinnamon sticks, sweet chili sauce, fish sauce, vinegar, and red wine in a saucepan, and bring to a boil, stirring. Boil for around 10 minutes, stirring occasionally, until lightly syrupy.

Prick the duck skin well, and heat the oil in a nonstick frying pan. Add the duck breasts and sear, skin-side down, for 8 minutes until browned, then turn and cook for another 8 minutes. Rest for 5 minutes before serving.

Cut the green onions into finger lengths, then into strips. Slice the duck thickly, arrange on warmed plates and scatter with green onion shreds. Spoon the sauce over the top, with the spices – for atmosphere, not for eating. Serve with rice or noodles.

SERVES 4

2–3 oranges

½ cup sugar

1 tbsp grated fresh ginger

1 small hot red chili pepper, finely sliced

2 star anise

2 cinnamon sticks

1 tbsp sweet chili sauce

1 tbsp Thai fish sauce

1 tbsp rice wine vinegar, or other wine vinegar

2 tbsp red wine or port

4 duck breasts, around 7oz each

1 tbsp vegetable oil

2 green onions, trimmed

Pancetta chicken

Wash and pat dry 8 large, boned chicken thighs. Mix
1 tbsp grated lemon rind with 2 crushed garlic cloves,
2 tbsp chopped parsley, sea salt, and pepper, and rub
into the inside of each thigh. Roll up and wrap in slices
of pancetta or thin bacon. Bake at 350°F for 45 minutes
or until tender. Serve on buttered corn kernels.

steak with mushrooms

Steak with mushrooms

A rich and creamy mushroom sauce smothers pan-seared steaks in a sort of beef stroganoff for the 21st century.

Cut the onion in half and slice finely. Wipe the mushrooms, discard the stems, and slice finely.

Melt the butter with the olive oil in a nonstick frying pan, and gently cook the onion for 5 minutes. Add the mushrooms and cook for 5 minutes. Add white wine, sea salt, pepper, and paprika, and bring to a boil, stirring. Reduce the heat and simmer for 5 minutes.

Heat a cast-iron grill pan or another heavy nonstick frying pan. Brush the steaks with a little olive oil and cook on one side, without moving, for 2 minutes. Season, turn, and cook for 2 to 3 minutes for medium rare. Season again, and leave to rest in a warm place.

Add the sour cream, mustard, tomato paste, and most of the parsley to the mushrooms, and cook, stirring, for 5 minutes. Place the steaks on warmed plates, spoon the mushroom sauce on top, and scatter with the remaining chopped parsley.

SERVES 4

1 onion, peeled

1 lb mushrooms

1 tbsp butter

1 tbsp olive oil

½ cup white wine

sea salt

freshly ground black pepper

1 tsp sweet paprika

4 boneless sirloin steaks, around 7 oz each, and 1 inch thick

3 tbsp sour cream or crème fraîche

1 tsp Dijon mustard

1 tbsp tomato paste

1 tbsp minced parsley

Grilled lamb and beans

The best way to get great-looking lamb chops is to buy a well-trimmed rack of lamb and divide it into 4 double chops.

Heat the oven to 350°F. Toss the cherry tomatoes and garlic cloves in 1 tbsp olive oil in a small roasting pan, and bake for 30 minutes.

Heat a cast-iron grill pan or the broiler until hot. Cut the rack of lamb into 4 double chops, and swipe them in the hot oil of the roasting tomatoes. Grill (or broil), skin-side down (or up), for 3 minutes, then for around 2 to 3 minutes on either side for medium rare, depending on size.

Drain and rinse the canned beans. Heat them gently with the remaining 2 tbsp extra virgin olive oil, sea salt, black pepper, and minced parsley. Divide among warmed plates.

Cut each chop in two or leave whole if you prefer, and arrange on the beans. Quickly toss the roasted tomatoes and garlic with the basil and spoon around the chops. Squeeze out the soft garlic from the skins to eat with the lamb.

SERVES 4

7oz cherry tomatoes

4 garlic cloves, lightly smashed

3 tbsp extra virgin olive oil

1 8-chop rack of lamb, well trimmed

16oz canned white beans (cannellini or flageolet)

sea salt

freshly ground black pepper

2 tbsp minced parsley

handful of basil leaves

Beef with shallots

My friends tell me that every time they cook this, their guests say it's just like eating in a restaurant. It is better than that, though. Restaurants don't give you second helpings of mashed potatoes.

Cook the unpeeled shallots in simmering water for 5 minutes, then drain and peel.

Heat the broiler, or a cast-iron grill pan or frying pan, until hot. Rub the beef with 1 tbsp olive oil, sea salt, and pepper. Broil or pan-sear the beef on all sides until well marked, but still rare inside, around 12 minutes. Remove from the heat and allow to rest for 10 minutes.

In the meantime, cook the potatoes in a pan of simmering salted water until tender.

Heat the remaining 1 tbsp olive oil in a frying pan, and fry the shallots for about 10 minutes until golden. Add the balsamic vinegar, and thyme and rosemary sprigs, and cook gently, stirring as the shallots color and caramelize.

Gently heat the milk with the smashed garlic until hot. Drain the potatoes and mash well, then beat in the milk, discarding the garlic.

Discard the string, slice the beef into ½-inch-thick slices, and season with salt and pepper. Spoon the mashed potatoes onto warmed plates and arrange the beef on top with the caramelized shallots. Scatter with parsley or chervil to serve.

SERVES 4
20 small brown shallots
1½ lb rolled beef tenderloin,
tied with string
2 tbsp extra virgin olive oil
sea salt
freshly ground black pepper
1½ lb red-skinned potatoes,
peeled
2 tbsp balsamic vinegar
few thyme and rosemary sprigs
½ cup milk
2 garlic cloves, peeled and
smashed
parsley or chervil sprigs,
to serve

Salmon in cabbage

An elegant way to serve an elegant fish for a dinner party or special meal. Easy, too, because you can package up the salmon beforehand, ready for steaming when you want to eat.

Peel off and discard the outer leaves of the cabbage, then carefully peel off 4 good, bright colored leaves. Drop them into a pot of simmering, salted water for 3 minutes, then drain and rinse under cold water. Shave off any inner ribs on the blanched leaves.

Trim the salmon fillets into neat squares, and remove any pin bones. Spread out a sheet of plastic wrap on a work surface and lay a blanched cabbage leaf on top. Place a salmon fillet in the middle, season well, and gently wrap the leaf around it to make a parcel. Wrap the parcel tightly in the plastic wrap. Repeat to make the remaining parcels, and chill.

SERVES 4

1 firm head Savoy cabbage

4 salmon fillets, around 6oz each, and 1¼ inches thick

sea salt

freshly ground black pepper

2 tomatoes

2 tbsp extra virgin olive oil

1 tbsp tiny capers, rinsed

1 lemon, quartered

Cut the tomatoes in half, and squeeze out and discard the seeds and juice. Mince the flesh.

Fill the base of your steamer with water and bring to a boil. Carefully remove the plastic wrap from the cabbage parcels, place them in the steamer, cover tightly, and cook for 8 to 10 minutes.

Gently warm the chopped tomatoes, extra virgin olive oil, and capers in a pan. Place the cabbage parcels on warmed plates and spoon the tomato salsa over and around them. Serve with lemon wedges and small boiled potatoes.

Teriyaki salmon

Japan's brilliant way with steak also suits the healthy richness of salmon. Serve on a snow pea salad for a crisp, fresh bite.

To make the teriyaki sauce, combine the sugar, sake, mirin, and soy sauce in a bowl, and set aside.

Wash and dry the snow peas, trim if necessary, then finely slice lengthwise into matchsticks, using the tip of a sharp knife. Mix the rice wine vinegar and sesame oil together in a bowl, add the snow peas, and toss until coated.

Remove any pin bones from the salmon fillets and pat dry with paper towel. Heat the vegetable oil in a heavy nonstick frying pan. Cook the fillets, skin-side down, for around 2 minutes or until the skin is crisp and you can see the flesh gradually changing color.

Turn the fillets and add most of the teriyaki sauce to the pan. Allow the sauce to bubble up around the salmon as you cook the other side for about 3 minutes, leaving the middle pink. (Don't allow to boil dry, or the sugar will burn.)

Divide the snow peas among plates and arrange the salmon fillets on top. Quickly heat the remaining teriyaki sauce and spoon it over the salmon to serve.

SERVES 4
8oz snow peas (about 1^3/$_4$ cups)
1 tbsp rice wine vinegar, or white wine vinegar
2 tsp toasted sesame oil
4 salmon fillets with skin, around 6oz each
1 tbsp vegetable oil

Teriyaki sauce:
1 tbsp sugar
3 tbsp sake (Japanese rice wine)
2 tbsp mirin (sweet rice wine), or sweet sherry
3 tbsp soy sauce

Swordfish with zucchini

Seared swordfish gets dressed up with zucchini and a lemony, herby Mediterranean dressing, known as salmoriglio. This is a great way to serve fresh tuna steaks, too.

Trim the zucchini, discarding the ends, then grate coarsely. Heat 2 tbsp olive oil in a nonstick frying pan and add the zucchini with sea salt and black pepper. Toss over a medium heat for 2 to 3 minutes until softened.

SERVES 4

4 medium zucchini

3 tbsp olive oil

sea salt

freshly ground black pepper

6 swordfish steaks, around
   6 oz each

4 caper berries, or a few
   extra capers

Salmoriglio dressing:

2 tbsp lemon juice

6 tbsp extra virgin olive oil

$\frac{1}{2}$ tsp sea salt

2 tbsp parsley leaves

2 tsp oregano leaves

2 tbsp capers, rinsed

Heat 1 tbsp olive oil in a nonstick frying pan. When hot, season the swordfish well and sear on one side until quite golden, about 3 minutes. Turn and cook the other side for another 2 minutes, depending on the thickness.

To make the dressing, whisk the lemon juice, olive oil, and sea salt in a bowl, and stir in the parsley, oregano, and capers.

Arrange the swordfish on a bed of zucchini and top with a caper berry or a few extra capers. Serve the dressing in a bowl, to be spooned on top.

Chili-basil mussels

Enticing, invigorating, exciting, and exotic, this is a great dish of Thai flavors for mussel lovers.

Scrub the mussels well, pulling out the little beards, and discard any that do not close when sharply tapped. Pick the basil and mint leaves from their stems.

Heat the oil in a wok, and stir-fry the garlic and ginger for just 30 seconds. Carefully add the wine and boil for 30 seconds, then add the fish sauce, chilies, and half the mussels. Cover and steam for 1 minute, shake the pan, then remove the opened mussels. Do this another two or three times, then discard any mussels that don't open. Repeat with remaining mussels.

Bring the broth to a boil, and add the chili sauce and most of the basil and mint leaves, stirring. Return the mussels to the pan, briefly tossing well over high heat. Scatter with the remaining basil and mint to serve.

SERVES 4
4^1/$_2$ lb mussels
bunch of basil
bunch of mint
2 tbsp vegetable oil
3 garlic cloves, peeled and smashed
1 tbsp minced fresh ginger
^{1}/$_2$ cup dry white wine
2 tbsp Thai fish sauce
2 hot red chili peppers, minced
3 tbsp sweet, seedy Thai chili sauce

Roasted tamari vegetables

Tamari is a Japanese wheat-free soy sauce with a deeper, more complex flavor than your standard soy. Use normal soy if you don't have it.

Heat the oven to 400°F. Cut the pumpkin into thinnish wedges, cut off the skin, and discard the seeds. Wash the carrots, peel, and trim the tops neatly. Peel the parsnips and cut lengthwise into quarters. Peel and halve the beets.

SERVES 4

1 lb piece of pumpkin

2 bunches of baby carrots

4 parsnips

4 fresh beets

2 tbsp tamari, or soy sauce

2 tbsp extra virgin olive oil

½ tsp sea salt

½ tsp freshly ground black
   pepper

handful of cilantro leaves

Dressing:

2 tbsp rice wine vinegar, or
   white wine vinegar

1 tbsp Thai fish sauce

3 tbsp extra virgin olive oil

1 tbsp sugar

Combine the tamari, olive oil, sea salt, and pepper in a big bowl, add the vegetables, and toss until well coated. Tip into a baking pan and bake for 45 minutes to 1 hour until tender and nicely browned.

To make the dressing, whisk the rice wine vinegar, fish sauce, olive oil, and sugar together in a bowl. Drizzle over the vegetables, jumble everything up a bit, and pile high on warmed serving plates. Scatter with cilantro to serve.

simple suppers

Penne with tuna

Cook little cubes of potato in the same pot as the pasta, and they'll be soft and lush by the time they hit the tuna and caper sauce. If you need an extra flavor hit, add a minced red chili pepper with the olives.

Peel the potatoes and chop into ½-inch cubes. Bring a large pot of salted water to a boil, add the pasta and potatoes, and cook together until tender, around 10 minutes depending on the pasta.

Drain the tuna, reserving the oil. Heat the olive oil in a pan, and add the tuna, olives, and capers. Toss well until everything is hot.

Drain the cooked pasta and potatoes, and add to the sauce with most of the tuna oil. Add the basil or arugula leaves with sea salt and pepper, and toss well over the heat until wilted.

SERVES 4

4 medium potatoes

1 lb penne or rigatoni

10 oz canned tuna in olive oil

1 tbsp olive oil

20 small black olives

2 tbsp salted capers, rinsed

small bunch of basil, or

    3½ oz baby arugula leaves

    (about 1 cup)

sea salt

freshly ground black pepper

Orecchiette with arugula

Finely slice 2 hot red chili peppers and 2 garlic cloves. Gently heat with 2 tbsp extra virgin olive oil in a big frying pan, stirring. Add 10 oz arugula leaves (about 3 cups) and toss until wilted. Add 1 lb cooked, drained orecchiette or similar pasta, toss well, and serve with grated parmesan.

Baked spaghetti

The good thing about this supper is that you can cook everything beforehand and put it together, then just bake in the oven when you're ready to eat.

Mince the onion. Heat the olive oil in a large frying pan and cook the onion for 10 minutes. Add the garlic and ground meat, and stir over high heat until it browns. Sprinkle with flour and cook, stirring, for 3 minutes.

Add the white wine and boil for 1 minute, then add the tomatoes, tomato paste, stock, sea salt, pepper, nutmeg, and rosemary sprigs. Partially cover and cook gently for 45 minutes.

Heat the oven to 350°F. Cook the pasta in plenty of boiling salted water until tender but firm. Drain well, then toss with the sauce. Scatter with parmesan, pile into a lightly oiled serving dish, and bake for 30 minutes until crisp on top.

SERVES 4
1 onion, peeled
2 tbsp olive oil
2 garlic cloves, peeled and crushed
1 lb ground pork, veal, or beef
1 tbsp all-purpose flour
$\frac{1}{2}$ cup white wine
28 oz canned crushed tomatoes
1 tbsp tomato paste
1 cup chicken stock or water
sea salt
freshly ground black pepper
$\frac{1}{2}$ tsp freshly grated nutmeg
few rosemary or oregano sprigs
1 lb spaghetti
2 tbsp freshly grated parmesan

chili-soy tofu

Chili-soy tofu

Even if you don't like tofu, you'll like this tofu. Serve with rice for a light, simple supper for two, or team it with the Asian omelet on page 143, or stir-fry duck noodles opposite, for a more substantial supper for four.

Fill the base of your steamer with water and bring to a boil.

Drain the tofu and place it on a heatproof plate that will fit inside the steamer. Steam the tofu for 20 minutes, then drain off excess water and carefully transfer to a serving plate.

Finely slice the red chili. Trim and finely slice the green onions.

SERVES 2

1 lb fresh tofu

1 small, hot red chili pepper

2 green onions

3 tbsp soy sauce

2 tsp toasted sesame oil

1 tsp oyster sauce

2 tbsp cilantro leaves

Heat the soy sauce, sesame oil, and oyster sauce together in a small pan until hot. Pour the mixture over the tofu, scatter with red chili, green onion, and cilantro leaves, and serve.

Stir-fry duck noodles

Oiled egg noodles, also known as Hokkien or stir-fry noodles, look like fat golden spaghetti. Asian food stores and larger supermarkets sell them. Pick up roast duck from Chinatown, or use leftover duck or barbecued chicken.

Remove the meat from the duck and finely slice it, discarding the bones. Mince the green onions, celery, and chili.

Heat a wok or frying pan, add the oil, and heat. Add the ginger and garlic, and cook until golden to flavor the oil, then remove and discard. Add the celery, chili, and half the green onions, and stir-fry for 2 minutes. Add the duck and stir-fry for 1 minute.

Put the noodles in a heatproof bowl, cover with boiling water, then drain immediately. Add to the wok and toss well over high heat.

Add the bean sprouts and toss, then add the rice wine. Add the hoi sin, oyster, and soy sauces, and toss well. Scatter with the remaining green onions and serve.

SERVES 4

$\frac{1}{2}$ roast duck (eg Chinese
roast duck)

3 green onions

2 celery stalks

1 small, hot red chili pepper

2 tbsp vegetable oil

1 slice fresh ginger

1 garlic clove, peeled
and smashed

14oz fresh oiled egg noodles

7oz bean sprouts (about
2 cups), rinsed

1 tbsp Chinese rice wine,
or dry sherry

1 tbsp hoi sin sauce

2 tbsp oyster sauce

2 tbsp soy sauce

Asian omelet

This works well with leftover roast pork, or barbecued Chinese char siu pork from Chinatown. It is also delicious with cooked shrimp or crabmeat instead of the meat.

Finely slice the roast pork. Rinse the bean sprouts in boiling water and drain. Wash the watercress, and shake dry.

To make one omelet, crack 2 eggs into a small bowl, and lightly beat in 1 tbsp rice wine, salt, pepper, and $1/2$ tsp sesame oil.

Heat 1 tbsp vegetable oil in a hot wok over high heat, swirling it around to coat the entire surface. Pour in the beaten eggs and quickly swirl to form an even omelet. Cook for 2 to 3 minutes until the egg is firm, then lower the heat.

Arrange some roast pork in the center, top with bean sprouts and watercress, and cook gently for a further 2 or 3 minutes.

Loosen the edges with a knife, then gently slide the omelet onto a warm plate, folding it over. Keep it warm while you make three more omelets. Drizzle with oyster sauce to serve.

SERVES 4
1 lb boneless roast or
barbecued pork
14 oz bean sprouts (about
4 cups)
7 oz watercress
8 extra-large free-range eggs
4 tbsp Chinese rice wine,
or dry sherry
sea salt
freshly ground black pepper
2 tsp toasted sesame oil
4 tbsp vegetable oil
4 tbsp oyster or hoi sin sauce

blue cheese potato

Onions with cheese

Everyone who loves baked onions calls this a great supper. Those who quite like them call it a great side dish for lamb, chicken, or steak.

Heat the oven to 350°F. Peel the onions and arrange them in a lightly oiled baking pan so that they fit snugly side by side.

Drizzle with the olive oil and bake for 1 hour until soft. Remove from the oven, and turn the heat to 425°F.

Combine the grated parmesan, nutmeg, sea salt, black pepper, and cream in a measure or bowl, stirring well.

Pour the cream over the baked onions, and sprinkle with paprika. Return the dish to the oven for about 15 minutes until the cheese sauce is golden brown and bubbling. Let stand for a minute or two before serving.

SERVES 4

8 medium white onions

2 tbsp olive oil

4 tbsp freshly grated parmesan

pinch of freshly grated nutmeg

sea salt

freshly ground black pepper

1 cup light or heavy cream

$\frac{1}{2}$ tsp smoked paprika

Blue cheese potato

**Put the spuds in the oven just before you go out for a quick
drink or an evening meeting, return an hour or so later, and
supper is almost done.**

Heat the oven to 400°F. Scrub the potatoes well and dry
thoroughly. Prick lightly, coat in olive oil, and roll in salt and pepper.

Place the potatoes on the rack in the center of the oven and bake
for $1^{1}/_{2}$ to 2 hours, until soft to the touch. (If you can hear them
softly whistle, they're perfect.)

Fry the bacon in a nonstick frying pan until crisp, drain well on
paper towel, and chop or crumble into shards.

Cut a cross in the top of each potato, and push in at the edges to
expose the inside. Pile the sour cream and blue cheese on top,
scatter with bacon and chives, and serve before it all melts.

SERVES 4
4 large baking potatoes,
around 8oz each
1 tbsp olive oil
1 tsp sea salt
freshly ground black pepper
4 slices bacon
$^{2}/_{3}$ cup sour cream or
crème fraîche
5oz Gorgonzola or Roquefort,
crumbled
2 tbsp minced chives
or parsley

Hash browns with bacon rolls

Plum tomatoes and honeyed bacon roast themselves, while you grate the potatoes and onion, and fry them into sweet-smelling, herb-strewn hash browns.

Heat the oven to 400°F. Cut the tomatoes in half lengthwise, season with sea salt and pepper, and arrange in a baking pan. Roll the bacon slices into tight rolls and place in the same pan. Drizzle bacon rolls with honey and bake for 20 minutes, or until the tomatoes are soft and the bacon is crisp.

Peel the potatoes and onion, coarsely grate them, then wrap in a clean cloth and squeeze out excess liquid. Place in a bowl, add the beaten egg, flour, chopped herbs, 1 tsp sea salt, and the olive oil, and stir well.

Heat 1 tbsp vegetable oil in a frying pan until hot, then add 2 heaped tablespoons of the potato mixture. Squash them flat and fry gently on both sides until golden brown. Keep them warm in the oven while you cook the remaining hash browns, adding a little extra oil to the pan each time.

Serve the hash browns topped with the roasted tomato halves, crisp bacon rolls, and rosemary.

SERVES 4

4 plum tomatoes

sea salt

freshly ground black pepper

8 thin slices bacon,
   halved if large

1 tsp clear honey

6 medium potatoes

1 small onion

1 extra-large free-range egg,
   beaten

1 tbsp all-purpose flour

2 tbsp chopped herbs
   (eg thyme, rosemary, chives)

1 tbsp olive oil

3 tbsp vegetable oil

rosemary sprigs, to serve

herby Potatoes, crisp honeyed bacon

warm, glowing spices

Sweet cinnamon, bitter saffron, nutty coriander, and floral nutmeg teach us to cook with all of our senses, adding warmth and perfume by the spoonful.

toast before use

There is nothing wrong with buying ground or powdered spices, but you will get more flavor if you buy whole spices and lightly toast them in a dry frying pan as you need them. Grind in an electric coffee grinder or pulverize with a mortar and pestle.

cinnamon coconut rice

Place 1²⁄₃ cups rinsed jasmine rice in a pan with 1¼ cups coconut milk, 1¼ cups water, salt, 2 cinnamon sticks, and 2 star anise, and bring to a boil. Cover tightly and simmer very gently, undisturbed, for 15 minutes. Rest for 10 minutes, then fluff up with a fork and serve with curry.

cinnamon toast

Mix 2 tbsp sugar with 1–2 tsp ground cinnamon in a jar. Toast bread under the broiler on one side, turn, butter the untoasted side, sprinkle with cinnamon sugar, and broil until melted.

sticky cardamom toffee syrup

Gently heat ³⁄₄ cup packed light brown sugar, 2 tbsp cream, 1 split vanilla bean, 2 tbsp butter, and 2 crushed cardamom pods until the sugar dissolves, then simmer for 5 minutes. Strain and serve over steamed puddings, cakes, and poached pears.

sweet, mulled wine

Combine 1 bottle light red wine and 1 cup muscatel wine or port with a split vanilla bean, 2 cinnamon sticks, 8 cloves, 2 bay leaves, and the rind of ½ orange. Cover and leave overnight to infuse. Heat gently, add 1 cup sugar, stirring, and serve warm.

clever with cloves

Strong little spikes of punchy flavor, cloves are the dried flower buds of an evergreen tree native to Indonesia. Stick them in an onion when cooking savory dishes, or an orange for sweet dishes, so you can take them out easily at the end.

grind your own nutmeg

Whole nutmeg is far superior to ready ground. Freshly grate or grind for cakes, soups, custards, quiches, and rice pudding.

the joy of red-cooking

Make a brilliant Chinese braise with 1 cup soy sauce, 1 cup chicken stock, 2 tbsp rice wine or dry sherry, 1 tsp toasted sesame oil, some fresh ginger and garlic, 1 tbsp sugar, and 3 star anise, and simmer for 10 minutes. Use it to poach Chinese mushrooms, chicken, fish, or pork, to serve with rice.

dip into Egyptian dukkah

In a hot, dry pan, toast $2/3$ cup sesame seeds, $2/3$ cup blanched almonds, $1/3$ cup coriander seeds, and 2 tsp cumin seeds until fragrant, stirring. Cool, then coarsely grind with 1 tsp sea salt and $1/2$ tsp pepper. Serve with warm Turkish bread and olive oil.

a great rice pulao

Fry 1 chopped onion in oil. Add 1 tsp each cumin seeds and brown mustard seeds, 1 cinnamon stick, 2 crushed cardamom pods, 1 bay leaf, salt, pepper, and $1/2$ tsp each ground coriander, cumin, and turmeric. Add $1\frac{1}{4}$ cups rinsed basmati rice and $2\frac{1}{2}$ cups boiling water, cover, and simmer gently for 15 minutes.

simple sweets

Rhubarb sponge pudding

The good thing about this pudding is that the rhubarb cooks itself under the golden sponge-cake topping.

Heat the oven to 350°F. Cream the butter and sugar together in a bowl until light. Add the eggs, one at a time, beating well. Sift the flour and baking powder into the bowl, folding it through quickly with a large metal spoon or spatula.

Cut the rhubarb stalks into $3/4$-inch lengths, discarding any leaves. Arrange in a tumbled fashion in a buttered 1-quart baking dish and scatter with the sugar.

Spoon the sponge batter on top of the fruit and bake for 50 to 60 minutes until the topping is a golden sponge cake and the rhubarb is tender. (If the topping appears to brown too quickly in the oven, cover lightly with foil.) Serve with rich cream.

SERVES 4
Sponge topping:
7 tbsp butter, soft
$1/2$ cup sugar
2 extra-large free-range eggs
$2/3$ cup all-purpose flour
1 tsp baking powder

Fruit filling:
1 lb ripe rhubarb stalks
$6^1/2$ tbsp sugar

Sugar plums
Brush 8 ripe
plums with beaten
egg white, then roll
in 3 tbsp white sugar to
coat well. Bake in a foil-lined baking
pan at 400°F for 15 minutes until
soft. Serve with mascarpone,
or the caramel yogurt on
page 175.

Banana ice cream

All the fun of banana ice cream, without the sugar,
eggs, or cream. Peel 8 firm, ripe bananas, wrap in
plastic wrap, and freeze overnight. Soften for 20 minutes,
then roughly chop and blend until thick and creamy.
Eat now, or refreeze, in which case soften
for 20 minutes before you slice or scoop.

Baked banana split
Bake 4 unpeeled bananas at 350°F for
30 minutes until the skin is black. Finely chop 4 oz
dark, bittersweet chocolate and 2 tbsp walnuts. Gently slit
the skin and peel back the top part. Scatter the split with
chocolate and nuts, then serve with ice cream.

Little lemon pots

Tangy little lemon custards can be baked ahead and served at room temperature, making them perfect for entertaining. You'll need 2 to 3 lemons, depending on their size. Serve with the coconut macaroons on page 182, for crunch.

Heat the oven to 325°F. Whisk the eggs and granulated sugar in a bowl until well mixed. Stir in the lemon rind and juice, and lightly whisk in the cream.

Skim off and discard any froth, then strain the custard into six 4-oz ovenproof ramekins or Chinese ovenproof white tea cups.

Stand in a shallow baking pan, and fill the pan with hot water to come halfway up the sides of the pots. Bake for 20 to 25 minutes or until the custards have set, with just a tiny wobble on the surface. Remove from the baking pan.

Serve the lemon pots either warm or at room temperature, dusted with confectioners' sugar.

SERVES 6

6 extra-large free-range eggs
1 cup granulated sugar
2 tsp grated lemon rind
½ cup lemon juice
⅔ cup light or heavy cream
confectioners' sugar for
    dusting

blood orange gelatin

Blood orange gelatin

As wobbly as a runaway bride, this do-ahead gelatin fills the mouth with its powerful tang. You'll need 3 to 4 blood oranges, depending on their size.

Put a few spoonfuls of the measured water in a small heatproof bowl and sprinkle with the powdered gelatin. Leave to soften for 5 minutes, then warm gently over a pan of hot water for about 5 minutes until dissolved.

Dissolve the sugar in the remaining water in a small pan, stirring, then bring to a boil. Remove from heat, add the blood orange juice, and whisk in the dissolved gelatin.

SERVES 4

1 cup water

1$\frac{1}{2}$ envelopes unflavored gelatin

1 cup sugar

1 cup blood orange juice

To serve:

4 slices blood orange

2 tbsp blood orange juice

Rinse four 4-oz molds with cold water, and shake dry. Fill the molds with the orange liquid, allow to cool, then refrigerate for several hours until set.

To serve, dip the base of each mold very briefly in hot water, run a knife around the edge to loosen the gelatin, and unmold onto a serving plate. Top each gelatin with an orange slice and drizzle with a little extra juice to serve.

Roasted vanilla peaches

One of the great quandaries of summer is whether to just devour all the glorious fruit, or whether to cook it. Here's one good, very simple, and deliciously fragrant reason to cook it.

Heat the oven to 400°F. Combine the white wine, sugar, cinnamon sticks, and vanilla bean in a small saucepan. Heat, stirring, until the sugar dissolves, then boil for 1 minute.

Place the peaches in a small, shallow baking pan and pour in the wine mixture. Bake in the center of the oven for 30 to 40 minutes or until the skins start to split, and the peaches look all toasty and flushed. Strain the juices into a pitcher.

Serve the peaches warm or at room temperature, drizzled with their cooking juices. If you have any summer berries around, warm them gently in the poaching liquid and serve with the peaches.

SERVES 4 OR 8
3 cups dry white wine
(1 bottle)
1 cup sugar
2 cinnamon sticks
1 vanilla bean, split lengthwise
8 firm, ripe peaches
handful of summer berries
(optional)

Little peach tarts

I don't believe these need either cream or ice cream, but feel free to disagree.

Heat the oven to 400°F. To peel the peaches, dunk them in a pot of boiling water for 5 seconds and the skins will peel off easily. Halve each peach, cutting around the side of the pit.

Roll out the pastry on a lightly floured surface and cut out eight circles, each 4 inches in diameter. Place on lightly oiled baking sheets and brush with beaten egg.

Place a peach half, cut-side down, on top of each pastry round. Drizzle the peaches with a little honey, and dot with butter. Bake for around 20 minutes until the peaches are soft and the pastry is risen and lightly scorched.

Using a warm spoon, drizzle a little more honey over each peach – this will glaze it beautifully. Serve warm or at room temperature.

SERVES 4 OR 8
4 large, firm, ripe peaches
1 lb puff pastry
1 egg, beaten
2 tbsp clear honey
1 tbsp butter, softened
1 extra tbsp clear honey,
    to serve

Moroccan rice pudding

A creamy, plump rice pudding, scented with cinnamon and fragrant orange-flower water – cooked in the pot.

Combine the rice, salt, milk, water, and cinnamon stick in a heavy-based saucepan and bring to a boil, stirring constantly to prevent the rice from sticking.

Reduce the heat and simmer at a gentle bubble, stirring from time to time, for 15 to 20 minutes or until the rice is plump, but the texture is still slightly runny.

Remove the cinnamon stick. Add the butter, sugar, and orange-flower water, and stir until dissolved.

Spoon the rice into warmed bowls and serve warm or at room temperature, dusted with cinnamon.

SERVES 4
$^3/_4$ cup arborio rice
pinch of salt
$2^1/_2$ cups milk
$^2/_3$ cup water
1 cinnamon stick
1 tsp butter
3 tbsp sugar
2 tbsp orange-flower water,
or rosewater
1 tsp ground cinnamon or
nutmeg for dusting

Gooey chocolate pudding

An oozy, boozy chocolate pudding with a soft, gooey – almost liquid – center.

Heat the oven to 375°F. Butter four 6-oz heatproof soufflé dishes or ramekins and place in a baking pan. Chop the chocolate roughly and melt in a heatproof bowl set over a pan of gently simmering water. Remove from the heat, stir well, and allow to cool slightly.

Beat in the vanilla, brandy, and sugar. Beat in the egg yolks, one by one, and then the flour. The mixture will be fairly stiff.

Beat the egg whites until stiff and peaky, then gently fold them into the chocolate mixture. Pour into the dishes and bake for 10 to 12 minutes until puffed and well risen. The puddings should still be gooey inside.

SERVES 4

1 tsp butter

5oz dark, bittersweet chocolate

½ tsp vanilla extract

1 tbsp brandy, rum, or Scotch

7 tbsp sugar

4 extra-large free-range eggs, separated

1 tbsp all-purpose flour, sifted

simple treats

Little chocolate cakes

If you can melt butter, you can make these cakes. Be brave and pull them out of the oven while they're still soft in the middle, for a dense, fudgy, heavenly treat.

Heat the oven to 350°F. Roughly chop the chocolate. Fit a heatproof bowl over a saucepan of simmering water, and combine the chocolate, sugar, and butter in the bowl. Stir as it melts into a smooth, glossy sauce. Remove from heat and cool for 5 minutes.

Add the ground almonds and stir well. Beat in the egg yolks, one by one, until well mixed.

MAKES 12

7 oz dark, bittersweet
  chocolate
½ cup sugar
½ cup butter
1 cup ground almonds
4 eggs, separated
confectioners' sugar for
  dusting

Place the egg whites in a large, dry bowl and beat until stiff and peaky. Stir a large spoonful of egg white into the chocolate mixture to lighten it, then gently fold in the remaining egg white.

Spoon the mixture into lightly buttered large muffin pans, or a 12-hole muffin pan lined with doubled muffin paper liners, and bake for 25 to 30 minutes.

Leave to cool for 10 minutes before removing from the molds. Serve at room temperature, dusted with confectioners' sugar, or store in an airtight tin for up to 3 days.

Caramel yogurt

How easy is this? Combine rich, thick yogurt with whipped cream, sprinkle with brown sugar, place in the fridge, and you have a luscious, caramel-topped creamy treat an hour later.

Whip the heavy cream in a bowl until peaky. Lightly fold in the yogurt, using a spatula or large spoon, then pour into a wide, shallow bowl.

Scatter the brown sugar evenly over the surface. Cover and chill in the fridge for 1 hour, until the sugar melts to form a caramel syrup.

When ready to serve, swirl the caramel sauce through the yogurt. Serve with poached fruits, pies, and tarts, chocolate cake, or as you would any rich cream.

SERVES 4
1 cup heavy cream
1 cup thick, plain, whole-
milk yogurt
3 tbsp dark brown sugar

Baby fruit cakes

These soft, fruity little cakes are so easy to make, it's almost spooky. Don't go on a picnic without them.

Heat the oven to 350°F. Combine the butter, raisins, currants, sugar, spice, cinnamon, ginger, baking soda, and water in a saucepan. Bring to a boil, stirring, then remove from the heat and allow to cool.

Add the eggs and beat well. Sift the two flours together, add to the mixture, and beat thoroughly.

Pour into lightly buttered or oiled muffin pans or a muffin pan lined with muffin paper liners. Bake for 30 minutes, or until a skewer inserted into the center comes out clean.

Allow to cool before removing from the molds. Store in an airtight container for up to 3 days.

MAKES 16
$2/3$ cup butter
2 cups golden raisins
2 cups currants
1 cup packed brown sugar
1 tsp apple-pie spice
1 tsp ground cinnamon
1 tsp ground ginger
1 tsp baking soda
1 cup water
2 eggs, well beaten
1 cup all-purpose flour
1 cup self-rising flour

my friend the friand

anytime shortbread

My friend the friand

The friand is a truly awesome small, moist, dense, rich, almondy cake. It's very, very French, and very, very chic.

Heat the oven to 400°F. Melt the butter and allow to cool, then use 1 tbsp to coat 10 muffin pans or individual oval baking molds, that are 4 inches long.

Sift the confectioners' sugar and flour into a bowl, and mix in the ground almonds. Lightly beat the egg whites with a fork, then fold them into the dry ingredients. Add the cooled, melted butter and lemon rind, and mix well.

Three-quarters fill each pan with the batter, and bake on the middle shelf of the oven for 10 minutes. Turn the pans around, and bake for another 5 to 10 minutes, until the tops are golden and spring back to the touch.

Leave in the pans for 5 minutes, then gently unmold onto a wire rack and leave to cool. Dust the friands with confectioners' sugar to serve, or store them in an airtight container for up to 3 days.

MAKES 10

$^3/_4$ cup butter (preferably unsalted)

$1^2/_3$ cups confectioners' sugar

$6^1/_2$ tbsp all-purpose flour, sifted

1 cup ground almonds

5 extra-large free-range egg whites

1 tsp grated lemon or orange rind

confectioners' sugar for dusting

Anytime shortbread

Free shortbread from the restrictively narrow timeframe of Christmas, and make it throughout the year. Hallelujah.

Heat the oven to 300°F. Combine the butter, confectioners' sugar, and sea salt in a food processor, and whiz until smooth.

Sift in the flour and rice flour, then pulse off and on, scraping down the sides from time to time, until the mixture gathers into a ball. Knead for a minute or two until smooth, then cut into two, wrap in plastic wrap, and refrigerate for 30 minutes.

Turn onto a floured surface and pat or lightly roll out the dough until $1/2$ inch thick. Cut into $1^{1}/_{2}$-inch rounds, using a cookie cutter or the rim of a liqueur glass. Reshape the scraps and cut more rounds. Place on a baking sheet and prick with a fork.

Bake on the middle shelf of the oven for 10 minutes, then turn the sheet around and bake for another 5 to 10 minutes until touched with color. Leave to cool on the sheet. Store the shortbread in an airtight container for up to 2 weeks.

MAKES 30
$2/3$ cup unsalted butter, soft
$2/3$ cup confectioners' sugar
pinch of sea salt
1 cup all-purpose flour
9 tbsp rice flour or cornstarch

Coconut macaroons

You can't get much simpler than this: three ingredients turned into crisp, little coconut cookies to serve with coffee, poached fruits, or the little lemon pots on page 160.

Heat the oven to 350°F. Whisk the egg whites, sugar, and coconut together in a bowl until they lightly come together. With wet hands, press the mixture into a flat, square shape, about $1/2$ inch high, on a board.

Cut out twelve 2-inch rounds, using a small cookie cutter or upturned liqueur glass, and place on a lightly oiled or nonstick baking sheet.

Bake in the center of the oven for 15 minutes until very lightly golden, just touched with color. Transfer the macaroons to a wire rack to cool. Store in an airtight container for up to 1 week.

MAKES 12
2 egg whites
$1/2$ cup sugar
$1^{2}/_{3}$ cups dried shredded
  unsweetened coconut

just egg white, sugar, and coconut

Espresso prunes

Dissolve 2 tbsp ground espresso coffee in $^1/_2$ cup boiling water, then strain. Add $1^1/_2$ cups sugar, 2 tbsp brandy, and 2 cups water, and bring to a boil, stirring. Add 1 lb large pitted prunes, and gently simmer for 30 minutes until the liquid is thick and syrupy. Serve with yogurt.

Chocolate bourbon balls

If you've ever made chocolate truffles, you will know they can be quite tricky. These aren't, but they are just as delicious. And if you're feeling elegant, decorate with edible gold leaf, available from cake decoration suppliers.

Finely chop the chocolate. Heat the cream in a saucepan, stirring until it bubbles, then remove from the heat, add the chocolate, and stir until melted.

Whiz the ladyfingers in a food processor, or crush with a rolling pin to fine crumbs.

MAKES 50

6 oz dark, bittersweet chocolate

$^1/_2$ cup heavy cream

8 oz Italian ladyfinger cookies (savoiardi)

1 cup confectioners' sugar

3 tbsp unsweetened cocoa powder

1 cup ground almonds

1 cup finely chopped walnuts

3 tbsp bourbon, or Scotch

$^3/_4$ cup butter, melted

unsweetened cocoa powder for dusting

Sift the confectioners' sugar and cocoa powder into a large bowl. Mix in the crumbs, ground almonds, and chopped walnuts. Add the bourbon, chocolate cream, and butter, and mix well.

Take a walnut-sized pinch of the mixture and roll into a ball in your hands. (If too wet, add a little more cocoa powder. If a little dry, add a dash more bourbon.) Place on wax paper on a tray, and refrigerate for at least 4 hours until firm. Roll each chocolate bourbon ball in cocoa powder to serve.

recipe index

index

cloves, 153

coconut macaroons, 182

coconut milk: cinnamon coconut rice, 152

   coconut shrimp with chili, 23

coffee: espresso prunes, 184

cookies: anytime shortbread, 181

   coconut macaroons, 182

   oatcakes, 21

coriander seeds: Egyptian dukkah, 153

corn: sweetcorn shot soup, 10

country terrine, 37

couscous with dates, 51

crackers: oatcakes, 21

crash hot potatoes, 99

cream: caramel yogurt, 175

   chocolate bourbon balls, 186

crostini, sweet onion, 28

croûtons, 80

crumbed goat cheese salad, 17

cucumber: fattoush, 74

   gazpacho with cucumber, 20

   parsley and lemon salad, 79

cumin seeds: Egyptian dukkah, 153

currants: baby fruit cakes, 177

custards: little lemon pots, 160

d

dates, couscous with, 51

desserts, 155–71

dinners, 89–107

dip, Egyptian beet, 39

dressings: salmoriglio, 126

   tomato vinaigrette, 86

dried fruit: baby fruit cakes, 177

drinks, fruity, 40

duck: Asian duck salad, 83

   chili-orange duck, 114

   stir-fry duck noodles, 141

dukkah, 153

e

eggplant and lamb, 98

eggs: Asian omelet, 143

   15-minute dinner, 111

   French café salad, 57

little egg and ham pies, 33

   spiced quail eggs, 15

   Tunisian salad pitas, 43

Egyptian beet dip, 39

Egyptian dukkah, 153

entertaining, 113–30

espresso prunes, 184

f

fattoush, 74

figs and baked ricotta, 38

fish: Chinese ginger fish, 106

   fast roast fish, 107

   herb crust, 47

   see also salmon

French café salad, 57

French onion soup, 110

friands, 180

fruit: herbs with, 46

   two fruity drinks, 40

fruit cakes, baby, 177

g

garam masala: chicken tikka, 91

gazpacho with cucumber, 20

gelatin, blood orange, 164

ginger fish, Chinese, 106

goat cheese: crumbed goat cheese salad, 17

   marinades, 47

   oatcakes with goat cheese, 21

gooey chocolate pudding, 170

green beans: French café salad, 57

   haloumi, tomato, and beans, 54

gremolata, potato salad with, 47

grill, mixed, 65

h

haloumi, tomato, and beans, 54

ham: 15-minute dinner, 111

   little egg and ham pies, 33

hash browns with bacon rolls, 148

herbs, 44–7

honey-soy quail, 63

i

ice cream, banana, 158

l

lamb: eggplant and lamb, 98

   grilled lamb and beans, 119

   lamb steak sandwich, 53

   marinades, 47

   parmesan lamb chops, 64

   Spanish meatballs, 61

lassi, 40

lemon: grilled zucchini salad, 69

   little lemon pots, 160

   parsley and lemon salad, 79

lemongrass: herb tea, 47

lettuce: chicken Caesar, 80

lime, caramel salmon and, 102

liver: country terrine, 37

lunches, 49–65

m

macaroons, coconut, 182

maple syrup: Amish pancakes, 31

marinades, herb, 47

mayonnaise: lamb steak sandwich, 53

meatballs, 47

   Spanish meatballs, 61

milk: Moroccan rice pudding, 169

mint: chili-basil mussels, 129

   herb tea, 47

   herby salads, 46

mixed grill, 65

Moroccan rice pudding, 169

muffins: beet burgers, 60

mulled wine, 152

mushrooms: chicken pies, 36

   steak with mushrooms, 118

mussels: Belgian mussels, 24

   chili-basil mussels, 129

my friend the friand, 180

n

noodles: beef sukiyaki, 95

   stir-fry duck noodles, 141

nutmeg, 153